How Much Joy Can You Stand?

Suzanne Falter-Barns

How Much Joy
Can You Stand?

How to Push
Past Your Fears
and Create Your
Dreams

BEYOND
WORDS
Publishing
I N C

Beyond Words Publishing, Inc.
20827 N.W. Cornell Road, Suite 500
Hillsboro, Oregon 97124-9808
503-531-8700
1-800-284-9673

Cover illustration: Betsy Everitt
Design: Lori Twietmeyer
Proofreader: Marvin Moore
Typesetting: William H. Brunson Typography Services
Managing editor: Kathy Matthews

Printed in the United States of America
Distributed to the book trade by Publishers Group West

Library of Congress Cataloging-in-Publication Data
Falter-Barns, Suzanne.
    How much joy can you stand? : how to push past your fears and
create your dreams / Suzanne Falter-Barns.
        p.   cm.
    ISBN 1-58270-003-6 (pbk.)
    1. Creative ability.   2. Creation (Literary, artistic, etc.)
I. Title.
BF408.F24   1999
153.3′5—dc21   98-47794
                                                           CIP

The corporate mission of Beyond Words Publishing, Inc.:
    Inspire to Integrity

In memory of my father,
John Falter,
who lived with joy

contents

how to use this book

THIS BOOK WAS WRITTEN IN RESPONSE to that creeping enemy of self-expression: entropy. If you've ever set out to create something, you know what I'm talking about, for sooner or later, no matter how well it's going, the whole damn system breaks down.

The book is organized into short, pungent little essays to read in such moments of flagging enthusiasm. Each essay is intended to inspire and help keep you going, despite the mental sludge.

Keep this book handy wherever you do the work of your dreams, and refer to its pages often. If this book does its job properly, you'll be up and running in no time.

why leap off the cliff
in the first place?

OF ALL THE BILLIONS OF PEOPLE who populate the Earth, you and you alone are capable of creating something unique. Whether it's the ultimate bagel, a thriving dry-cleaning business, a lifetime of exquisite tapestries, or a child, you are the only one who carries the blueprints. This is the gift you have been given, and if you've ever listened to that small, still voice in the dark recesses of your soul, you know this is true. Somewhere in there, the longing to manifest this gift speaks to you on a regular basis; it's that embarrassing dream you keep coming back to, the one that usually feels so hopeless.

The purpose of this book is to explore the one thing necessary to move you toward that dream—your own creative process. So why does there need to be an entire book about the creative process? Because without it you may never realize any of your dreams, whether that means becoming a fine artist, playing pro ball, or managing a mutual fund. Your creative process informs every decision you make, from conceptualizing, problem solving, and networking to trying to decide which emotion to express. Creativity is not the lone province of artistic types with dirty fingernails and picturesque garrets. Rather, the creative process is a lifeblood we all share—a fundamental human skill with millions of applications. It is essential to accomplishing anything in life that's uniquely your own; it is the engine that drives your dreams.

Unfortunately, there is one small problem. Out there right now, circulating around the atmosphere, is a carload—an eighteen-wheeler load, really—

of out-and-out lies about creativity. And if you're trying to pursue any kind of dream, you can't help but get run over by it once in a while. Hopefully, armed with enough information and clarity, you can dodge those madly careening trucks and see your way to the other side. I wrote this book in an attempt to prevent further road kill.

I figure that all the lies surrounding this process have persisted because we're basically a doubting, disbelieving breed. We have to make up whatever thoughts we can to keep us from doing the work of our dreams, and so the myths persist. In nearly twenty years of my own creative work, many of them spent encouraging others to express themselves, I've seen more people cling to more lies that render them absolutely powerless than I ever thought possible. Yet, these lies are nothing but leaky life rafts, for they only prop you up for a while before giving out entirely. Furthermore, they're no substitute for swimming. Whether you admit it or not, that dream of yours isn't going away. Far from it, it will badger you relentlessly until you finally give in and listen.

Look at the dogged persistence of your dream, the way it keeps on chattering at you, regardless of how often you shove it aside. Look at how it reappears at odd, restless times—the middle of the night, or those first crystal-clear moments of the day—whenever you're unusually lucid and your mind is free of clutter. Look at how that voice carries on year after year, decade after decade, growing fainter at times and stronger at others, but still refusing to die altogether.

It is almost as if we cannot bear these precious, private visions. The very presence of a dream is incredibly threatening, for to actually follow it implies a freedom we think we do not have—not now, not here, not in this secure, comfort-lined world we've constructed to be as seamless and mindless as possible. Pursuing the dream would mean too much hard work, too many demanding hours, less security, less television! Worst of all, it would mean exposure, and even more mortifying, *potential humiliation.*

Yet far more devastating has to be that withering moment at the end of a life when you look up and realize you've missed your chance. You settled for mediocrity and will now die alongside all of that unrealized potential, and because this really is the end of the road, there will be no going back. You will have blown it, big time, for once and for all.

What is mind-boggling about this scenario is that it happens at all, for the pursuit of a dream is actually a simple, straightforward affair. Pursuing dreams requires bravery, discipline, patience, and ingenuity, yet these are qualities every one of us possess—*if* we're willing to do the hard work that dreams demand, *if* we're willing to honor our creative process instead of fighting it.

Creativity is the magic seed that we automatically assume we were born without yet that is lying latent, waiting in every single one of us. This book is about tending that seed so it flourishes as effortlessly and as naturally as God, Brahma, the Universe, or whoever originally intended. And because most of us regard creativity as a temperamental, whimsical, all-too-fragile breeze that may or may not blow in our direction, this book is intended to smash all those myths about it as well. The fact is, your creative instincts are a lot like your underwear; they're right there in the drawer waiting for you to climb into them every day. They are not fragile and temperamental, nor do they play favorites. In fact, your instincts are on call whenever you need them—as long as you remember to reach for them. That's really all you need to know.

Well, OK, you say. But why bother with all this dream-pursuing, creative hoo-ha in the first place?

Simply because of the joy.

If you can manage to leap off the cliff and trust yourself to fly, you will experience a fine, effortless joy like nothing else. You will experience a larger connectedness with the Universe and, possibly for the first time, see your place and your own unique value in it. You will be doing what you were always intended to do, and this is the secret of the whole process. For once you've truly tasted that fantastic fruit, there is literally nothing, not even years of flat-out rejection and failure, that can keep you from its magic. The process of creating the dream becomes too pleasurable to resist.

It may take a while to wade through all your resistance, fears, misperceptions, and basic disbelief in yourself—it may take far longer than you think it should. But if you can just go through the process and trust yourself in a basic way not attempted before, the joy will be yours. Like a muscle, your vision and creative instincts will become stronger, clearer, and more vital each time you connect with them. Your commitment will strengthen, and with it, the world will cooperate in ways you never would have expected. Little signposts will appear along the way, offering support and encouragement. People will show up, bringing challenges, ideas, or information. Your dream will begin to materialize, the result of nothing more than finally listening to the still, small voice within.

It is out of my love for this perfectly simple design that I wrote this book. It is also out of my love for you. Joy is available to all of us, right this minute, here and now, forever and ever.

All you have to ask yourself is this: How much joy can you stand?

try this...

When the raw stuff of dreams begins to collect, you might want to store it all somewhere. Sprinkle a handful of blank notebooks throughout your life for jotting down ideas and inspirations. Keep a small tape recorder on hand for recording observations. Buy some large plastic boxes for keeping bits and pieces of the raw materials your dream demands. Then designate a specific place for this important cache: the piano bench, an empty closet, or the bottom drawer in your desk.

Once you've begun to collect ideas, materials, and odds and ends that pertain to your dream, feel free to dig in frequently and create. The fact is, the more you write, record, and accumulate, the more power you give to your vision.

Now get out there and have fun.

dare to be heard

SO YOU WANT TO BE A VENTURE CAPITALIST, write a screenplay, or open a Victorian tea garden like the one you visited once in London and have never forgotten. So you want to do anything slightly risky that demands a personal vision.

You? . . . You? says the voice, as it collapses on the floor in gales of laughter. *Who do you think you are, anyway?*

For many of us, this is where the conversation about pursuing our dream begins and ends—because, let's admit it, we're sensible people. We're not the sort who take huge, wild risks. Furthermore, we're not the slightest bit visionary. We don't have a lot of high-minded thoughts that keep us awake at night, and God knows we don't know the first thing that those other, more successful people must have known before they set off to realize their dream. We're just . . . us. Basic. Flawed. Certainly nothing special.

Actually, when you get right down to it, we don't really even deserve to have a dream.

Still, we do have this niggling idea that keeps surfacing and resurfacing, begging to be explored, teased out, played with, and realized. We, otherwise staid individuals, do have to admit to oddly ambitious stirrings not completely understood. So we do what we have always done: we ignore them.

After all, we're just not the kind of people who go off half-cocked after some so-called dream. Right?

The truth is that people with creative impulses need to create, no matter how "uncreative," sensible, logical, and otherwise unimpulsive they consider themselves. People with a pressing idea have an obligation to express it. And yet we almost never do. What prevails is a weirdly common belief that no one wants to hear what we have to say. No one wants to know about our great new idea, patronize our business, attend our productions, or give us any kind of a break. *No one.* We think the world is just waiting to flatten us with some great universal sledgehammer.

This is the soft, dark underbelly of all dreams, the part that's hovering in the shadows, hoping to derail you. And this is the first and seediest demon you will have to confront. The really annoying part is that the demon is you. All that imagined rejection is nothing more than your own twisted imaginings. When examined in the cool, rational light of day by other, more benevolent people, your own contribution usually merits a much greater response than you could ever imagine.

I will never forget the first time I performed my cabaret act—a two-woman show in which my partner and I wrote and sang all our own music. For months and months we'd worked on the act, composing, harmonizing, writing lyrics, choreographing moves, all the while convinced that what we were doing was good but strange. No one in their right mind was actually going to like this stuff, though we might get some polite applause. In fact, we only kept going because we were having fun.

Then our opening night rolled around. As we stood on the stage singing our first number, a curious thing happened. People began to smile. They nodded and sat up a little straighter as if they were actually listening, and then a miracle occurred: they laughed. All of them. Loudly, even. The audience got the first joke in the lyrics, then another, and another. They laughed in places I hadn't even anticipated. Like some fantastic flying machine lumbering into that sacred moment of lift-off, the act was working. At that moment, I fully understood the impact of what my partner and I had created, and it shocked me. I was someone worth listening to. People actually wanted to hear what I had to say.

The common disposition among us is a painful sort of shyness. People get embarrassed when called forth to be themselves for even a millisecond in front of others. The core belief is that since nothing I say matters to anyone, I will end up looking like a dork. This is the precise feeling that keeps people from feeding their dreams.

Oddly enough, that sniggering voice of doubt never really goes away. Years go by and you get somewhat used to it. You learn to test the waters more and more, and eventually the voice slides from an obnoxious bellow into more of a background drone. Witness the famous Sally Fields acceptance speech on winning her second Oscar: "I guess you really do like me, don't you?" Observe the fact that Truman Capote was once quoted as saying he'd never written anything he thought was *really* good. Not even *Breakfast at Tiffany's.* Jane Austen wrote of her work, "I think I may boast to myself to be with all possible vanity, the most unlearned and uninformed female who ever dared to be an authoress."

The point is this: No matter what you take on, insecurity is part of the job description. It's not possible to blaze new trails and forge your own path while remaining on familiar ground. If you want to start a business, you take on financial risk. If you want to move to another part of the country, you plunge yourself and whoever is attached to you straight into the unknown. If you want to try any endeavor you care about, you're going to have to kick it out of that cozy little nook it has carved in your soul. And you're going to have to stand there and watch your dream as it takes its first baby steps. This is not an experience for people who crave comfort.

Writer Raymond Carver likened publishing his stories to riding at night in the backseat of a driverless car with no lights on.

And yet, such vulnerability can be a valuable part of the creative process. An acting teacher I once knew insisted that serious doubt is actually a very good sign, a signal that you're being completely honest and vulnerable in your work. Mark Twain said of *The Adventures of Huckleberry Finn*, "I like it only tolerably well ... and may possibly pigeonhole it, or burn the manuscript when it is done." As for me, I got through the first novel I published only by convincing myself that no one would ever read it. I was sure that this was yet another little piece of my own personal weirdness that no one would ever have to sit through. Yet a major publisher actually bought it.

Daring to be heard, then, is simple. It's recognizing your cascades of self-doubt for what they are: a whole lot of hot air you've cooked up for absolutely no good reason at all. Then it's mustering up the courage to trust yourself for five minutes anyway, because maybe you really do have something important to say. And, ultimately, it's having one of those defining little epiphanies and saying, "What the hell." Daring to be heard means recognizing that if you put your voice out there, all you're going to get back is a yes or a no. The days of public stoning are long over; so is being pilloried. In fact, a large part of the world won't even be paying attention, no matter how loudly you scream.

Daring to be heard, ultimately, is something great you do for yourself. It's giving your poor, withered soul some fresh air and sunshine. Daring to be heard means stretching out languorously in the luxury of a strong opinion or basking in the joy of planning an endeavor you've always wanted to start. No matter what your medium, the dream is yours and yours alone to realize in your own particular way. With the dream comes the chance to represent yourself in the world in a way that truly matters. And so daring to be seen and heard becomes the chance for perfect freedom.

It becomes your chance to fly.

try this...

Take a pad of paper and a large, fat magic marker (big, black, and permanent works wonderfully well). Unplug the phone, get family and roommates out of the house, and close your door. Then spend the next half hour gloriously scrawling out whatever opinion or idea or invective you've wanted to hurl in your life but didn't. Pick a person you should have spoken up to but didn't. Then scribble it all out on that pad, as fast and furiously as you can. Don't stop. Don't judge. Don't even think. Just spew. If you run out of paper, get more! Just keep on going until you've said everything you have to say to as many people as you can think of. If you find yourself crying, yelling, and pounding the pillows on your bed, all the better.

I find this exercise to be particularly useful after stressful family visits or bad days at work.

how to get the fire in your belly

FIRST OF ALL, THE TITLE OF THIS CHAPTER IS DECEPTIVE. There really is no "way" to get the fire in your belly about anything, much less the arduous pursuit of a vision. The fire is born through solitary activity requiring not only balls-to-the-wall honesty and extreme patience but also the willingness to chip away for years at work that the world at large may never even see.

Passion is an elusive beast, and it appears to land on certain people almost whimsically, through some act of God. This explains how a fifty-five-year-old New York City doorman I once read about in *The New York Times* was able to put himself through law school at night—a task that included an average of four hours of sleep a night for six years—while the rest of his buddies were content to open doors for the rest of their lives.

The difference between him and the other doormen was not the dream, for you can be sure he wasn't the only guy opening doors for executives with expensive suits and heavy briefcases and fantasizing about what their lives were like. The difference was that this doorman chose to act, and not only did he choose to act, he chose to do it *no matter what*. The fact that he had to live on next to nothing for years while he paid for his education didn't matter. The fact that he studied until one o'clock every morning and then got up at five for work didn't matter. The fact that he was the only person in his class with gray hair and middle-aged spread didn't matter. Even the fact that he was looking at a career shortened by age didn't matter. What mattered to him was one thing: the single and absolute pursuit of his dream. He was going to be a lawyer, *no matter what.*

Not surprisingly, after sending out more than a thousand résumés, he was hired by an associate who was impressed by his tenacity and passion. "I may not get more than ten good years from him," he said of the former doorman, "but they're going to be ten excellent years."

What this story has to do with the getting of passion is everything, for passion isn't something one "gets" at all—it is something one merely allows. That doorman knew he wanted to be a lawyer, and so he stepped out of the way and let his desires take over, no matter how much work that entailed. He didn't doubt, he didn't avoid, he didn't fill the world with a carload of sputtering excuses, and he didn't sweat the details. He merely let this wild, riderless horse take him on a fantastic ride toward the horizon while he simply surrendered. He listened, he heard, and he said yes. His willingness was truly stunning.

For every person in the world who pursues their dream, there are hundreds, if not thousands, who talk about it constantly. They make lists of great book titles and accumulate impressive amounts of sheet music. They stand around at cocktail parties regaling whoever will listen about an idea they have for the next big market phenomenon. Or they are perennial students who see themselves as having to study well into the next century before they can ever fully know their craft. And for every one of these people, there is a small, fitfully started, precious piece of work in some forgotten corner of their desk.

In that drawer, there is an abandoned beginning, evidence of a wonderful moment when their head and heart filled to a point they could no longer stand and they had to sit down and work. Ideas poured out of them, thoughts congealed wondrously, everything made fantastic sense, and like the March children under the influence of pixie dust, suddenly they could fly.

However, the tragedy happened the next morning. Flush with the false impression that it would always be so easy, free, and liberating, they now expected a daily miracle. Yet creativity, like life, is never predictable. What happened was they had to sit and think for a while. Then they sketched out a few ideas they hated, erased them, and drew up an entire page of ideas they hated. Next the phone rang and they avoided the subject altogether for a good half hour. And when they finally looked at what they'd accomplished that night, they had little more than one flimsy page of mediocre work.

"*Proof!*" screamed a voice out of nowhere. "*That's* proof! *This dream business is totally out of control. What do you think—you're Donald Trump or something?*" Back to good old comfortable resignation. Back to hanging out. Back to the tube and a Bud. In other words, back to reality.

The truth is if there had been a third night, a fourth night, and a hundredth night, that precious piece of work might have turned into something great. The creative process is not computer software that provides all the answers at the click of a mouse. Rather, the process is a mysterious beast who comes to sit by your side and befriend you only after you've stroked and fed it every day for a long, long time. This beast demands your care and nurturing, it wants to build up your trust, and it craves your love, because in truth, that beast is only you.

More people don't create than do because they cannot give themselves that critical extra bit of love. They lie terribly to themselves, insisting that they can't do it, deciding that they haven't got anything worthwhile to say, pretending that their dreams don't matter. But these dreams do matter, desperately. Every unpursued dream leaves the world a tiny bit paler, and life a little less rich. Every untold story means one less lesson passed on to someone else. Every abandoned idea means one more strike against hope.

A fire in the belly is a champion for the ridiculous. You must keep on going day after day, stroke after stroke, step after step, simply because you have to. You have to, in order to honor yourself—a ridiculous notion in a world that values products more than people, and the bottom line more than somebody's tender dreams.

The fire in your belly comes only when you're willing to work at your dream for no good reason. You don't pursue the dream because you'll be famous someday, because the work is going to make you rich, or because you'll make better cocktail banter. You design, teach, invent, or serve because this is what you are meant to do.

Getting the fire in the belly means simply surrendering to the truth.

try this...

You have three minutes. Make a list of everything that you are truly passionate about. List anything you can think of, from eating imported chocolate to having great sex to fly fishing on the Snake River. Then think about what characterizes those experiences. Do you go into a trance and lose track of time? Does the experience leave you feeling like a better, stronger person? How often do you let these passions into your life? Are there any you need to pursue now?

can it really be so simple?

I WOULD LIKE TO SUGGEST SOMETHING RADICAL.

What if that movie you've always wanted to make, the one you've spent hours silently directing as you chugged home from work on the train, the one you've often fantasized about devoting entire vacations to but still haven't written a word of, the one you just *know* Jodie Foster would agree to star in, was already made? What if the movie was sitting out there in hyperspace, fully formed, just waiting for you to calm down enough to sit down, listen up, and start typing? What would you think?

Initially, you would probably think I am nuts. And yet, I say it is entirely possible.

Inspiration is delightfully unexplainable. The closest any of us can come to naming its source is to say we honestly have no idea. Yet whenever you get yourself to sit down for a moment and actually listen, something is usually right there in front of you, waiting to be expressed. Of course, the tricky part isn't expressing, it's listening.

Often in the past, when I sat down to do something creative, I would hear an absolute cacophony of marching orders: *OK, smarty pants—think of something. You're not thinking of anything . . . What's the matter, Stupid? . . . Don't use that idea—that's as old as the hills. Who wants to hear about that? Come up with something better—now . . . See? (Sigh.) . . . Pitiful.*

It was like trying to compose a symphony in the middle of a jackhammering construction site. So no wonder it takes people years to get to the point where they actually sit down and start something.

What one is forced to do, ultimately, is surrender. Meditation helps significantly. But the single, biggest inroad comes when you learn to accept the fact that those snarling pit bulls in your head will always be there, on the attack, ready to destroy whatever fragile endeavor you set out to pursue. They will continue to insist that what you have designed, planned, or invented isn't really exactly right. They will demand that the project be redone hundreds of times until your precious creation is as limp and chewed over as a dead dishrag. And they will have you convinced that nothing you do, *nothing*, will ever amount to a hill of beans in this world. And it won't— if you listen to them.

First, you have to see these voices for what they are—a mere smoke screen set up to distract you. A meaningless test, as it were. Then you must simply allow the voices to do their thing and understand their presence as an integral part of your creative process. Undoubtedly, the voices will blabber on for a while as you valiantly hang in there, trying to hear the feeble cries of creativity behind all the fracas. Over time, though, the pit bulls will subside. Their protests will gradually grow shorter and shorter as the voice of your work becomes louder, and you will begin, ever so slowly, to see the value of your undertaking.

So eventually, when you listen, you will hear more and more input that is productive. And while you may be deeply suspicious that creativity could be so simple, you begin having more fun, and so you go with it. Fairly soon, you will be able to sit down and actually tune out the pit bulls and tune in the creativity channel directly. And so, finally, you can begin to listen in earnest.

By listening selectively, you will tap into that greatest of all possible teachers: your instinct. While you may study technique, have the help of big-time professors and consultants, and get lots of pointers on how to use your tools, nine-tenths of your creative work still comes directly from your gut. So when you quiet your mind and concentrate hard enough, the guidance is usually there, turning your hand this way and that, moving you to blend unexpected colors. It takes you down alleyway after alleyway and into the offices of people you'd never expect to meet. It catapults you into entirely unexpected landscapes again and again and again. And all because you've simply learned how to listen.

At such times, this process can feel almost as if you're entering a trance, for when one is truly engaged in any creative act, day-to-day, mundane thoughts melt away as one begins to work. A more powerful force takes over. The simple expression of the soul pours through mind and body as time disappears. Work is completely absorbing. Then you happen to look up and notice that three hours have gone by, and what you've created is pretty damn great. And that's when you know bliss.

Of course, mistakes are an important part of the process, too. God knows, I've gotten it wrong more often than right. Yet the beautiful thing is that those mistakes are usually guided. They're simply part of the creative journey called "my own line of cosmetics" or "some recipes that will eventually be a cookbook." The mistakes simply become part of the work unraveling, prompting you to retackle whatever went wrong until eventually, after extensive reworkings, you hit it dead on.

If you are patient enough and work and work at your dream, always striving to be utterly faithful to your voice and your path, you will eventually succeed, for you will have brought into being that elusive image you've been carrying around in your head for far too long. You will have given birth to a great, creative wonder and can now reap the joys of parenthood.

It really *is* this simple—the work is out there, waiting for us to heed its call and fall under its spell. Conveying your dream requires only this: your listening heart, give or take nothing.

try this...

If one must have a headful of snarling pit bulls, one might as well schedule them. Pick a time each day when you plan to do your work, and allow the first fifteen minutes strictly for the pit bulls. In other words, schedule your screaming self-doubts right into your work session. Give them lots of room to really raise hell, and try to sit back and observe while they do. You might even write down a few of the more choice ones. Then, once these voices of doubt have had their rant for the day, they should go away and mind their own business, leaving you free to get busy.

the end of struggle

SOMEWHERE, A LONG TIME AGO, someone decided that great works aren't truly great unless they have been suffered over copiously. Writers should drink heavily and gnash their teeth when they write. Ballerinas should bleed. Entrepreneurs should spend every last penny they own and then work like hell while digging themselves deeper into debt. For creativity to be valid, it has to be soaked in fresh struggle.

Balderdash.

What makes a ballet wonderful or a business take off is the simple outpouring of the creator's soul. And if this person is truly doing his or her job, the process will involve an immense amount of effort but not a whit of struggle. Effort is the clear-minded application of one's abilities, while struggle is nothing more than a whole lot of unnecessary lather.

It's like this: You decide to open a great little Italian restaurant. You've got your chef lined up, your investors loosely in mind, and you've done the business specs and found that there's a legitimate need in a certain part of town for decent Italian. You've even gone to the extra lengths of getting a few of the old family recipes from your cousin in Naples and a hot tip on where to buy superb extra-virgin olive oil in bulk. So you're off. Every day after your regular job, you start to put in a little time on the restaurant.

Within a few months, two investors are on board, and though you still need a third, you begin to look at rental properties and talk to designers. Day one, day two, day three, day seventy-five pass. You continue to make progress, albeit slowly. Some days go spectacularly; others don't.

Just when you find the fabulous little storefront of your dreams, with exposed brick walls and an incredible kitchen, one of your investors drops out, claiming he's overextended. But then another backer miraculously shows up a week later, and he's got a cousin at the Liquor Control Board. You sweat, plan, crunch numbers, and dream. You keep finding recipes and talking to your chef. You're on the verge of signing a lease when disaster strikes again: your other original investor quits, citing tax problems.

About this time you have lunch with a friend. He asks you how it's going, and you say, "Fine, thanks. It's harder than I thought it would be, but I'm getting there." He asks, "How long until you open?" You answer honestly, "Six months, a year. Who knows? I just lost an investor." A worried look passes across your friend's face, and you can feel your quiet reserve of strength suddenly becoming marshmallow-like in your gut.

Enter struggle.

"Bummer," he says with concern. "Yeah, I know," you sigh as you stare at your lunch. Other restaurants seem to spring up overnight and are started by people with money to burn—no one is more aware of that than you. Silently, you begin to wonder if maybe this restaurant thing isn't such a wild idea to begin with.

At this point you have a choice. You can look at your progress as lousy and something to obsess about, or you can see it as part of a larger process over which you have little or no control. You can choose to struggle or you can simply forge ahead and open the restaurant.

If you are a struggler, you will begin to brood over whether this project is "really happening" or not. In very little time, your mind will become a cluttered mess of conflicting messages with emergency alarms going off all over the place as the once clear and beautiful voice of your project slowly withers away, unable to be heard.

The dream may go unpursued then, until you realize that this work is a unique creation, unlike any other one you or anyone else has ever attempted, and so it may take a little longer. In fact, your dream may take a *lot* longer. Yet that's no reason to quit. If anything, it's the reason you need to get right back to work.

The point is this: Your work, in and of itself, does not demand struggle. Your dream demands discipline, honesty, patience, enormous effort, and a fair amount of heart. It demands that we give of ourselves or not even bother. And it demands that we love life and people enough that we wish to give back the gift we were given. That is all the work requires.

Struggle, on the other hand, is something people bring to the party—one of those quotidian, human responses, like the urge to tear open someone else's pile of birthday presents. And ultimately, struggle is really nothing more than a complaint, a way of saying, "I don't want to work this hard, therefore let me make a major drama out of it and maybe I won't have to." Basically, struggle is your ego having its nasty little way.

And actually, when you are truly connected to what you should be doing, struggle is the furthest thing from your mind. All you really want to accomplish is the task set before you, and you'll do pretty much anything to make it happen. Look at Gun and Tom Denhart, who started the children's clothing company Hanna Anderson in their living room. The Denharts' mission was to re-create the high-quality, 100 percent cotton children's clothing from Gun's native Sweden for American consumers. They were so dedicated to communicating the quality of their fabric that they personally cut and glued one-inch squares of the material into seventy-five thousand catalogs themselves. For the Denharts, this was just another labor of love, a natural part of building a business that only eleven years later earned $50 million in revenues.

Struggle is the refuge of people who cannot face their own brilliance, people who, for whatever reason, must stay hidden away at all costs. They're the wannabes who diligently sign up for classes but stop coming halfway through. They're the dabblers who start a million projects but never finish any of them. Or they're the people who simply refuse to stick with anything they care about, who suffer from anorexia of the spirit, which they bandy loudly about them in an attempt to appease their wounded hearts. Just like the rest of us, these people sorely wish their work to be loved, so much that they can't even show it to the world.

Yet at the same time, struggle should not be confused with the need to take a break. Sometimes, after you've patented sixteen inventions in a row, it might be appropriate to take a few months or even a year off. Still, there is no need for struggle. You can simply realize that the work may not be flowing for a reason—sheer and simple exhaustion. And then you can begin the process of refueling, observing, and allowing yourself plenty of unstructured time to do nothing more than daydream and wonder, which in turn becomes a different sort of creative act.

There is so much sweetness to be found in the disciplined doing of your work. It is an undramatic, everyday sort of life, but so rich and full of pleasure that after a time you cannot *not* do it. What is there for you is simply the uncovering of yourself an inch at a time, the finer, better part of you that knows no limits and wishes only to share its own intrinsic genius. This is the part of you that knows the joke about struggle.

The strugglers work hard at struggling; the rest of us work hard at our work.

try this...

Take a pad of paper, and at the top write "Good Reasons Why Not." Then list every single excuse you've used to avoid pursuing your dream. Make sure it's an exhaustive list. Really think about it—take a few days to be certain it's complete. Then put the list away for at least one week.

Schedule a time (and write it in your book) when you will look at this list again. Make sure you are free of distractions and interruptions when the appointed hour arrives. Sit down with your list, and go through each excuse. Then, with every ounce of honesty you've got, cross out every excuse that you know in your heart is bogus. Be relentless. The amount of honesty you bring to this step will determine the exercise's effectiveness.

You will be left with a handful of items on the list that are your karmic lot in life. If you want to pursue this dream, you'll simply have to deal with them.

On the other hand, you will finally understand that you do, indeed, create your own destiny.

vulnerability for the faint of heart

I AM A PERSON WHO HAS NEVER BEEN COOL. Although I devoted about three-quarters of my life to the pursuit of cool, it just never jelled. I was always too tall, too awkward, an emotional slob, and worst of all, I was constantly being told that my speaking voice sounded exactly like Miss Jane Hathaway's on *The Beverly Hillbillies*. I couldn't imagine a less cool person to be compared to.

Somewhere in the vicinity of thirty, I gave up. What prompted this was that I finally walked away from a long, fairly tortured relationship. The minute I dredged up enough courage to leave, my entire existence changed. Suddenly my life went from being about the pursuit of cool to being about the pursuit of nothing. It was as if I had been stripped clean. After all the tears and regrets, all I was left with was my plain, old, unglamorous self.

So every night after I came home from my job writing toothpaste commercials for a big ad agency, I'd take out a pen and a notebook, and I'd sit on the couch and wait. Slowly, Miss Jane Hathaway would come creeping back. The voice of my inner self, that tender, emotional, wiser, more real other person would begin to express herself, and I'd find myself making notes. As if by magic, the changes I was going through found their way into words, and these words began to be song lyrics.

Though I'd always sung in an on-again, off-again way, I'd never written a song in my life. Yet now I found myself hearing quasi-melodies and rhythms; verses somehow snapped neatly into place. Without knowing how, why, or even what, exactly, was happening, I became a songwriter. And what was driving those songs was an entire aspect of myself I'd always longed to express but never had.

Eventually, I began to feel the tiniest urge do something with the stack of songs on my desk. But what? Obviously, I wasn't a *real* songwriter—I was only someone who'd written a few songs that were probably not only terrible but completely ridiculous. At least that's what my thinking process told me. Still, the small voice within kept on demanding I take them out into the world. But how? I didn't have melodies for them, so what was I supposed to do? Call up ASCAP and plead my case? Stand on the street with a sign saying "Songwriting Partner Wanted"? God knew I wasn't about to do something serious and official like run an ad. I ended up doing the only thing I could think of: I went to a psychic.

The psychic was amazingly straightforward about it. "What are all these songs, and why are you hiding them?" she demanded. She went on to describe a collaborator for me in detail—a tall jazz pianist and composer who was a friend of someone I knew. We would have an uncommonly good vocal blend if we chose to sing together, she said. Three weeks later, I was sitting in the apartment of a tall jazz pianist and composer introduced to me by a friend. This woman's understanding of my lyrics was so full and precise, and her music for them so achingly beautiful, that the only thing I could do when I heard them was cry.

There I was, the tall, skinny, vulnerable me, written out in chords that expressed something deep and essential I'd always wanted to say. There was the voice I'd been shutting up for all these years, finally given some room to breathe. Here was an entirely new and rich way to bring myself forth in the world. I was amazed, moved, and suddenly filled with passion. My scribblings really were songs after all, and not only that—they were good! Getting the songs out there suddenly became the most important thing in the world to me. It was as if, for the first time, I felt myself to be as completely and fully alive as God intended.

Carey and Falter, the act that our songs turned into, never played Carnegie Hall, but we did play New York's small, back-room cabarets for a wonderful three-year run. We developed a small following of core devotees who never missed a show. We lost money and worked our hearts out, practicing between three and four hours every night after our jobs. We infuriated our bosses, confounded our boyfriends, and worried our parents, but we couldn't have cared less. For two young, restless women in their twenties, this undertaking became an act of pure and wonderful defiance, a thousand defining moments squeezed into one forty-five-minute cabaret act. And what this had to do with vulnerability was everything.

In our own minds, we were flying high without a net. And although neither of us had ever done anything like this, we operated with a weird sort of confidence—the same confidence children display when they learn how to ski: they don't think or analyze. They just point the skis down the hill and go, usually in a straight line. So it was with our act. Whenever a question came up, we'd just look at each other and operate on instinct. We were completely and totally in what the Zen Buddhists call "beginner mind." Because we didn't realize how little we actually knew about creating a cabaret act, we acted with a marvelous, creative certainty that came entirely from our guts.

Furthermore, we were completely passionate about our work, driven by the delicious freedom of expressing our true selves for a change. There was joy to be found in even the most mundane technical rehearsals and midnight stamp-licking sessions. We'd already done the hard part, coming out of our own particular closets, so now the rest of our work was painted with the pure and simple happiness of doing what we were truly meant to do.

What we learned was the power of our voices—not our singing voices, which did, in fact, blend uncommonly well—but our *voices*. Our presence. Our essences. We discovered that we had weight in the world and that the simple sharing of ourselves, our true selves, was in and of itself quite moving.

When the author Frank McCord won the Pulitzer Prize for *Angela's Ashes*, he told *The New York Times*, "I learned the significance of my own insignificant life." It is a shock when you realize the value your own inner secrets hold to others. Yet it is true. The public wants to be moved, delighted, and struck by your bravery. They want to see you succeed, and they crave your initiative. If you are an artist, people long for the depth of your expression; if you are a businessperson, they hope to be inspired by your vision and creativity. And no, the public doesn't want the canned version of a good idea—they want *your* good idea, the one that can only come from your own particular set of DNA.

When you think about the great success stories through history, every one of them came about because someone was dreamy enough to think they could actually do something in their own weird way. Consider Benjamin Franklin, Abraham Lincoln, and Bill Gates. Lincoln did not free the slaves and Gates did not start Microsoft because it was the easy thing to do. Franklin did not run around in a rainstorm hoping to attract lightning for kicks. These men did these things because the small, still voice demanded they must.

Every one of these people embraced their own vision, saw the perils, and leapt anyway. They didn't sit around licking their wounds and guarding their most intimate feelings. They probably didn't even consider their feelings, or they never would have leapt at all. And they certainly didn't fret over outcomes like being electrocuted or starting a war. Being truly vulnerable means having uncomfortable feelings, facing risks, and barreling ahead anyway. Vulnerability means plunging headfirst into the fear, the uncertainty, and the great stew of the unknown for no good reason other than it's what you have to do. Vulnerability means allowing yourself to take on the difficult and rise to the occasion. You assume these challenges not because you ought to or because of some guarantee that everything will turn out OK but simply because you must.

And here is the wonderful payoff you receive in return: the secret of real vulnerability is that it becomes your greatest source of strength.

Once you're out there in the thick of it, the tender part of you that so feared public excoriation will rise up bigger, better, and stronger, ready to do anything to defend the honor of your endeavor. This is all the support and brilliance you will ever need, for unbelievable fortitude, determination, and bravery will seem to come from nowhere. And yet it will come from you, a natural and powerful aspect of yourself that has always been there, even if previously asleep. Like a muscle, your vulnerability strengthens with use, melding into your core beliefs about yourself and feeding your reserves. And slowly, the walls of steel behind it will reveal themselves—walls of steel you probably never even knew you had.

At adventure programs all over the country, people pay large sums of money just so they can tap into these reserves while hanging upside down off a belay line forty feet above ground. Such reserves are real and present in every one of us, yet the only way to reach them is straight through your tenderest parts.

It is not until the beast is unleashed that it can prove its speed, and so it is with the power of your dreams. It is not until you take on risk that you will find out what you are truly made of. And believe me, you're made of far more than you think.

In your vulnerability lies not humiliating goofiness but that divine thread which links us all together. In your vulnerability also lies your power. Simply put, it is where all dreams truly begin.

try this...

Find some old photographs of yourself, preferably from your most awkward, zit-riddled teenage years, or even earlier, when you were still a wild, free little being, full of thoughts and feelings.

Do not choose pictures in which you're smiling politely for the camera. Choose the ones where the camera caught you unguarded and exposed. Choose photographs that remind you of a time and place that mattered deeply to you, an experience that can still stir your emotions when you look at the pictures.

For maximum effect, make oversized copies of the images. Then hang these pictures in the place where you do the work of your dreams.

where to look for inspiration

INSPIRATION IS EVERYWHERE. Most of the time, though, we can't see it. And it isn't even that we don't look; rather, we don't know how to look.

We are living in an era that lacks gratitude. Humor is ironic; disillusionment is the status quo. To wander outside and spend a moment enjoying how softly the snow outlines a sapling is considered a pretty pointless, nerdy thing to do. To be hip, you must be fast, furious, and powered up by the latest technology, whether it's antidepressants or computer modems. There is no time for reflection, so don't even bother. "What's it going to get you?" goes the popular thinking.

No small part of our dilemma comes from our addiction to things—sneakers that flash, toys that beep, a ceaseless parade of gadgets that all seem designed to counteract each other. These are short-lived technologies, all of which are around to keep us entertained, distracted, totally comfy, and ultimately, utterly bored. Like television, new technologies provide us with too much stuff to contemplate, and so we contemplate nothing. We walk outside to *get* somewhere instead of simply taking a walk.

Yet it is in such simplicity that ideas live. I live in New York City precisely because I can step out my door and be bombarded with sensations, feelings, spectacles, and insights. Recently, someone left an old upright piano in front of the empty lot across the street from our apartment. In the space of one short day, I saw someone doing t'ai chi next to it in the rain, a very large man doing a Jelly Roll Morton impression for his laughing wife, and a very somber little girl in a Christian Dior coat playing "My Country 'Tis of Thee." A week later, someone came along and smashed the piano into smithereens. The following afternoon, the scrap-metal man came and cut off all the strings, and his friend, the scrap-lumber man, took the wood. It was the life and death of an abandoned piano, in three short acts. I never could have written it so perfectly if I'd tried.

There are tremendous riches around us all the time, but we must tune ourselves in to seeing them. Imagine how it is when you live near a mountain. Every time you see it, it seems completely different. Sometimes the mountain is blazing gold, burnished by a brilliant sunset. Other times it is a forbidding block of black on the horizon, and it appears truly menacing. Still other times, the mountain can be the palest lavender, baby pink, or soft gray after a snow; sometimes it disappears altogether in a storm. Our view of the mountain is continuously changing, and one can never predict what it will look like next. From this perspective, the view out your window becomes even better than television for pure, spontaneous entertainment.

The natural world, whether it's the haphazard poetry of city street life or the scattering of autumn leaves in a mountain forest, is the single, greatest creative resource we have. The workings of the world are seemingly random, yet the interplay is fantastically complex and perfect. Whether you believe in God or not, you can't help but find inspiration in the chaos of life. It is here, in plain, old, boring "everyday" reality, that the best ideas begin. As the old chestnut goes, you've got to use what you know.

To do this, then, begins with gratitude. You've got to perceive of the life that unfolds around you as the rich source of information that it is. You've got to look at the perfect upheavals, coincidences, and crises of your life and the lives around you as what they really are—truly miraculous. You have to cut the stifling back-chatter about "my painfully boring existence" and begin to plumb it for raw material, for this is where you will find the solutions to a million different creative problems and possibilities. You will find a treasure trove of connections and vast networks of supporters. You will uncover stories that have to be told and opportunities that must be seized. Such rich material will not be far away and unreachable but literally right in front of you.

All that has to be added is your particular take on all this raw material. In fact, this is what makes any creative work great—the presence of you in the act of creation. It was Beethoven's massive fury with his growing deafness that made his most important symphony, the Ninth, the masterpiece that it is. Edward Hopper was unafraid to convey the isolation not only in his own life but in everything around him, which he painted with unflinching dedication. Carolyn McCarthy, who was a registered nurse until her husband and her son were shot on the Long Island Railroad, was unafraid to take on gun-control laws, which landed her in the House of Representatives. Each of these people was committed to one thing: giving us their take on the world, as honestly and fully as possible. And that is why their work endures and succeeds and continues to make an enormous difference today.

The world really does want to know what you think. All you have to do is tell the truth—your truth—in all its glory. If you see unfairness and injustice, then that is what you must express. If you see rage dissolve into sweet forgiveness, then that must be your message. If you see a better way to make a mousetrap, then you must make it. Whatever it is that speaks to you must be passed on to others. That is your responsibility as a member of society.

As Bruce Springsteen once said, "If you're an artist, you try to keep an ear to the ground and an ear to your heart." Well, the same can be said for all of us. Here is where you will find true inspiration.

try this...

Make these lists:

Ten Things I Love About My Life
Ten Things That Are Uniquely "Me"
Ten Things I Know That I'd Like to Share
Ten Things I Could Fix or Change in the World

try this, too...

Use a camera (disposable or real) and begin to shoot pictures of people, places, and events that are evocative for you. These should be places you'd like to keep a little piece of because they move you. Have the film developed and place the photographs in an album or a box, any place where you can visit them frequently and have your juices stirred a bit. When you're feeling uninspired and your dream seems dead in the water, take a look at your pictures.

the boring truth about living your dream

THERE IS THIS MISPERCEPTION OUT THERE that if you want to pursue your dream, you have to know exactly what you're doing. Just look around at all those other, more successful people out there. They move through life with a crisp smile and an unwrinkled shirt, and when you ask them how their work is going they always say the same thing: "Great!" It's actually kind of nauseating.

But the truth is that none of us ever fully know what we're doing. We make projections, lists, sketches, and plans, but things seldom go as we wish. Life is unfortunately unplannable; it's a fluid, random conglomeration of stuff, people, conditions, attitudes, needs, ideas, and circumstances that careens down the road like an overloaded wagon, ready to mow down anything in its path. So you have to be ready to leap out of its way at any time and pull your project to safety along with you.

That's when you wind up by the side of the road, licking your wounds and cursing your decision to get involved in the whole thing in the first place. Then you remember how little you know. And then you think about how much all those other people seem to know. Finally, you remember how insecure this whole situation feels. And then, well, hell, why not just quit? After all, if you want to make your dream work, you have to know what you're doing. Right?

Absolutely, categorically, unequivocally wrong.

The very nature of creating something is that you almost *never* know what you're doing. Sure, you know some technical stuff and you can put together a reasonable-looking product. Sure, you know most of the steps involved. That's the easy part. But the real meat of the creative process, the inspiration that will set your project on a path of its own, is far more complex and elusive than that.

The popular belief is that inspiration "strikes" us like a lightning bolt from the sky. Actually, it's the other way around. In reality, we strike inspiration much the way miners strike gold. By ceaselessly working, reworking and reworking the old territory, sooner or later we'll run into a little nugget of something wonderful, something better. The more we dig, the more we'll find until—if we're very lucky and very persistent—we hit the mother lode. In reality, creative work is no different from swinging a pick. For every day of incredible divine intervention, there are probably ten spent sifting through the dirt.

This is the bad, boring news about going after what you want: just like any job, there are many times when the work is unexceptional, difficult, and downright demanding. Yet these are also the days when you hunker down and keep on doing because there simply isn't any other way to get where you're going. And herein lies the difference between the average dreamer and the person who goes after their dreams. The successful person is willing to put up with the hard work because inside of it he finds a joy like nothing else on earth. But the average dreamer does not know this joy yet. The average dreamer finds his joy in tangible rewards and gets stopped when he realizes all that hard work may ultimately "be for nothing."

When you set out to undertake the work of your dreams, it is critical that you understand something: the reason so many people abandon their fledgling musical comedies, antique stores, and medical careers is because they expected it to be perpetually fun and interesting. "But this is my dream!" they think lustily. "It *has* to be fun." Then the minute the dream gets challenging, which it inevitably does, they quit, as if it suddenly turned into the wrong

40

dream, or more likely, as if there were something wrong with them—some weird defect all those other, more successful people never, ever suffer from. In fact, there isn't a thing in the world wrong with any of these people; it's just that they don't understand that pursuing your dream takes effort. *And just because it takes effort is no reason to abandon it.*

Each day spent digging puts you that much closer to the gold. And over time, if you keep at it, a curious thing happens: you begin to love sifting through the dirt. Some of your happiest moments can come during the seventh and eighth rewrites of a novel, when you're reinventing your character's peculiar walk for the umpteenth time. Happiness can come in the small hours of perpetual sanding you've put in on a fine piece of furniture, when the wood grain begins to be as smooth as silk and you begin to feel the rightness of what you set out to do. Finally, you can understand all those curious twists and turns you took and see the larger, greater picture that they form. And this is when all your doubts about your goal begin to blow away like so much dust in the wind.

This is also the point when you come close to sensing the divine in your work. It does not arrive heralded by trumpet-blowing cherubim, or even in a seamless blast of nonstop inspiration. Rather, the divine steals over you in the small, humdrum hours of your undertaking—during the checking, refining, editing, and polishing. The divine creeps in during yet another unexceptional night in your workroom, exactly when you least expect it.

As you climb inside the fantastic nautilus of your creation, you begin to understand why Zen masters spend entire lifetimes perfecting the tea ceremony. It is the sheer poetry of creating something from nothing and working on it until it is truly and absolutely right that ultimately keeps you coming back.

This is the magic that can only be born of hard work, and this, ultimately, is realizing your dream.

try this...

Buy or create an oversized calendar for your dream and hang it in the space where you do this work. Make a mark on each day that you actively work at your project. You can add qualifying remarks, describing how the work went, or any other notes pertinent to your process. You can go the kiddie-reward route and paste on Superman stickers or gold stars whenever you've pressed through a lot of resistance or managed a breakthrough. You can cut out and tack up faces from magazines and catalogs that describe the emotional climate of each day's work. Or you can write and stick up one-word descriptions summarizing poems or quotations on self-adhesive notes. The important thing is to put a little bit of yourself on this calendar each day that you work at your dream.

Your calendar should be a big, visual journal of the pursuit of your dream, a constant reminder that you are giving yourself an important gift and that you are, indeed, making progress.

how to pray and work at the same time

BY NOW, I CAN HEAR WHAT YOU'RE THINKING.

Sure, you make it sound easy—but this is not *going to be easy.*

But I haven't got *any intuition!*

How am I supposed to know what's emotionally honest and what isn't?

But I really *haven't* got any time—really!

HELP!!!!

First of all, remain calm. Or perhaps, more accurately, try to get calm. Calmness, in fact, is essential to this entire process—calmness, plus trust in that key element, yourself.

I guarantee that your intuition is there, always has been there, and always will be there. But you're not going to find it until you become still and learn how to listen. Then, and only then, will you begin to hear your inner guidance at all and tap into your own vast wellsprings of trust. For me, this has been accomplished a number of ways, the most important being through meditation.

By meditation, I don't mean anything particularly mystical, nor do I mean the "right" way to meditate as opposed to the "wrong" way. What I mean is methodically stilling the voices in your head for even a few minutes every day—whether it's first thing in the morning, on the train while coming home from work, or whenever you can grab a regular bit of time. Meditation could mean silently counting to yourself as you rhythmically inhale and exhale. It could mean finding a mantra, a meaningful little phrase or affirmation that you chant or repeat silently to yourself. It could mean staring into a design or the flame of a candle. Meditation could also mean prayer, a walk in the woods, feeding the birds, or having a long, thoughtful run. You must experiment and play with the calming process until you find whatever is inherently right for you. What is important is the stillness you create and the regularity with which you do it.

What will happen as you meditate is that life itself will become increasingly quiet. The nervousness of the everyday with all its attendant anxieties will take a new place, subordinate to the great reservoir of calm you are now building at your center. From calmness you will be able to access all those lovely creative juices, and the more you plumb its depths, the greater this resource will become. Ultimately, you will find that the work itself becomes the meditation, putting you directly in touch with your spiritual connection almost every time. Like some character out of the Bible, you will be doing what you do not because it brings home the bacon but because it has a higher, spiritual purpose. You will, indeed, be heeding your calling.

So once you've gotten in touch with all this lovely, spiritual energy, you must make room for it often—every day, if possible, through both your meditation practice and regular work on your dream. Please notice that I'm not talking about that other, more mundane work you've filled your life with up until now. What I'm talking about is soul work, the pursuit of which every day, or nearly every day, fills your life with incredible equanimity and joy. Like chocolate cake, the more you taste it, the more delicious it becomes until, quite literally, you simply can't resist.

It is precisely this deliciousness that leads people to give up their jobs on Wall Street to become sheep farmers, or to sell the split-level in suburbia and head off to serve in the Peace Corps in Bosnia. There is a sense of rightness about your dream, and the more you allow this feeling into your life, the stronger it will become. This could be the reason so many people shake their heads regretfully and mutter, "I could never be that disciplined." What they're really saying is, "I could never allow myself to wake up and hear the calling I've been successfully ignoring for years."

It's as if we can't bear to be that good to ourselves. It's as if we've always been told to keep it small, to carve out only a modest chunk of satisfaction for ourselves. Whether or not you believe in God, your meditation will serve you by honoring that lost piece of your self. And once honored, that self will not sit silently by. For this reason, such regular scheduling should never be seen as "having discipline," that militaristic-sounding condition that makes pursuing your passion sound like some sort of bondage and deprivation. Rather, all it really means is giving your soul a little space to fool around every day, and that so-called discipline will magically turn into freedom.

What is obvious to me is that we avoid our creative undertakings simply because we've lost touch with that other, more powerful part of ourselves. We think that we haven't got any intuition, or if we do, it's flawed. We think that we're too busy to bother listening. We insist that there really is no possible space we can work in, or that our toddler, aging mother, needy spouse, or frantic boss are more deserving of every spare minute we have than we are.

Our heads are filled with animated conversations about why we can't stop to feed our passion instead of why we can. We're convinced that our circumstances are different. *Really! Honestly! They are!* We insist that we are special and that we, and we alone, are the only people on the planet to whom none of this applies. We're convinced that there's never enough time, money, or inspiration to do the work, or that there's no point because "none of it will ever see the light of day, anyway." We're convinced that no one will give a whit about what we want to contribute. Most of all, we're convinced that we're right.

What we've forgotten is that this work is prayer, and I don't necessarily mean the religious version which happens in a church or a temple. Pursuing

45

the dream is the prayer of simply living as we are meant to live. Inherent in this is the understanding that we are not alone but are connected to the pull of the Universe, for it is in our work that we can finally surrender into God's infinite and comforting embrace. Doing our work means realizing that we do not know all the answers and then relaxing blissfully into our semi-ignorance, simply doing what God has given us to do.

So there is more at stake here than the swing of your moods and whether you'll ever actually get down to work. What pursuing your dream is really about is your place on earth and the benevolent demands of your own personal version of God.

The world awaits your vision. So when will you find it in yourself to share?

try this...

Begin to walk. I have found that a long walk the first thing in the morning clears my head and supports my own work incredibly well. And by walking, I mean moving at a brisk pace for at least twenty minutes in comfortable shoes, down a road or around a neighborhood that offers some kind of pleasure. You can take a walk to work or a meander through a country field; choose the same route again and again, or vary it, depending on your mood.

As you walk, use the time to access God, or whomever you recognize that great big protective force to be. I find myself giving thanks and having conversations. Sometimes I make up a short affirmation and repeat it in rhythm with my steps. Sometimes I just daydream, and as I do fine ideas for my work come along. Whatever the case, I hope you find, as I have, that these spiritual walks feel so wonderful you just can't not do them. (Note: See "A List of Inspiring Books" for some books on walks of this type.)

Do this every day or as often as you can. Your work should blossom accordingly.

expect a miracle or two

THERE COMES A MOMENT IN THE MIDST of every creative project when the whole damn thing looks impossible. The moment usually arrives when you're on a roll, busily generating ideas and feeling the fun straight down to your toes. It is that terrible moment when you realize you cannot go another step until you've located another half a million by next Friday or wangled an hour-long interview with Salman Rushdie on film. Damn your good ideas. What only a moment before seemed like a happening, no-problem project now, in an instant, has become blatantly impossible.

This is where commitment comes in.

Commitment is not some coat you put on and take off depending on the weather. It's a promise you make to yourself that must be renewed every single day, and always in the context of work. In other words, you sit down, you do the work, and you thereby reaffirm your commitment. If the work has taken a hold of you, you *have* to reaffirm it—it's unavoidable. You may find yourself thinking about your project at odd moments. A bridge for a song might come while waiting in line for a bagel; a sudden solution to a marketing problem might happen in the bath. You find yourself living your project in a most natural but unexpected way. And in your commitment to it, you find yourself solving the impossible.

Yet commitment also happens on days when such solutions are not flowing. Then you sit with yourself for a while, computer glowing quietly in front of you, waiting and listening. A few false starts might come along. You'll come up with a few ideas that don't feel particularly connected to anything, so you'll erase them. Then more silence. You might be tired that day, or simply needing a break. And ultimately, you'll take it. You simply can't solve the problem on this particular day, but you don't worry. You know that your commitment isn't going anywhere; you know you will be back in that chair the next day, waiting and probing for more wonderful stuff. Having an off day does not in any way affect your overall dedication to the project. And this is where the miraculous part comes in: miracles do show up, almost as rewards to your commitment.

One day, while working on a novel, I wrote myself into a corner when I decided one of my characters had to make cream of truffle soup shortly before he killed himself. Now, anyone who's been around truffles knows that these exotic mushrooms are hard to find, having a season of about fifteen minutes during which they are uprooted by trained pigs, and so they are also hellishly expensive. Still, having never tasted a truffle, I realized I couldn't write about one until I had. The problem was that all I had to spend on this particular research was a twenty, even though a healthy bunch of truffles runs somewhere in the three figures. Still, off to the local gourmet grocery I went, dubious but willing to try.

I arrived just as the black-truffle season was sputtering out, so the person behind the counter offered me white truffles in a jar, in the precise quantity I was looking for. "How much?" I asked. He inspected the jar. "$23.50," he replied. Amazed and relieved, I told him to wrap them up, which he was doing when his boss appeared and much whispering ensued. The young man seemed crestfallen as the boss walked away. "What happened?" I asked. He looked at me dolefully. "The price was actually $235.00," he said, "but since I quoted you the lower price, that's all you'll have to pay." Miracle achieved, research accomplished.

Now, I don't mean to get dangerously cosmic here and suggest that all you have to do is wish for something and it will magically appear on your doorstep. But it is my belief that if your path is straight and true, and you're really listening to your instinct, the world will fall in line to support your dream, no matter how outlandish your needs may become.

It is almost as if the world wants us to succeed on our chosen path and will do whatever is necessary to point us on our way. The story is told that Grandma Moses painted her first large painting because she was wallpapering the living room and ran out of wallpaper. Using the brush she'd painted the floor with, she created a quick landscape of butternut trees by a sunny lake and put it up to cover the gap. A relative loved it and began to encourage her, and so her work as a fine artist began in earnest.

My husband, Larry Barns, realized his dream of buying a New York City apartment building even though he didn't have nearly the money such a purchase usually demands. Still, he found a building whose price had been slashed twice, since all the tenants were striking and a squatter had taken over the owner's apartment. Everyone he went to for advice told him not to buy the building—and a crooked estate lawyer demanded cash in a paper bag just to show it to him. He couldn't even get in to see all the apartments because the tenants had changed the locks. Still, after two years of looking he knew this was the building he wanted, in spite of its many problems.

Larry went ahead and bought the building anyway. As it turned out, the tenants ended their strike after he sat down with them and gave them new leases. The squatter turned out to be his old girlfriend, a woman he'd been living with a year earlier who'd moved out one day, unannounced, and disappeared. When she found out who her new landlord was, she not only gave up the apartment willingly but sat down with him and had the talk that completed their relationship. And so Larry ended up with the building he'd always dreamed of at a price he could afford.

The founder of Sears, Richard W. Sears, began his business while he was employed as a freight processor at the Minneapolis and St. Louis Railroad.

One day an unclaimed shipment of watches turned up. After a few weeks, it began gathering dust in the claim room, so the enterprising Sears did a little market research, found out the wholesale costs of the watches, bought the freight himself, and began selling watches up and down the railroad line. This led to his forming the R. W. Sears Watch Company. Interestingly, the watchmaker who originally did all the watch repairs for Sears was Mr. Roebuck, so eventually the company took the name Sears, Roebuck & Company.

The point here is that quirks of fate are part of the plan. Complete happenstance, lucky coincidences, and total accidents *do* occur and for good reason. I believe such occurrences aren't really accidents at all but rather are traffic signs giving you the right of way. They happen almost as rewards to your single-minded dedication to your project, showing up to affirm your path and to give you that little goose of encouragement you've been needing.

I know that someone somewhere is reading this right now and saying "Yeah, *right*! I'm gonna decide I need half a million and it will just magically show up in front of me . . . What kind of fruitcake book is this, anyway?"

Here's all I have to say to that: Bend your imagination a little. So what if this is only my opinion and not some scientifically proven fact? Such thinking can only help you with your own particular vision. One of the things I love most about life is what a mystery the human brain is. The truth is, we really don't have any idea how these so-called coincidences occur—whether we have some sort of extrasensory skills that can predetermine them, whether they really are acts of God, or whether they are completely without meaning.

The key is to receive such synergy as a gift, for if nothing else, it will provide critical ballast the next time your impetus begins to sag. "Hold fast to your dreams," said Walt Whitman.

And while you're at it, expect a few miracles, say I.

try this...

Before you decide that you're one of those people for whom miracles never happen, pull out your journal or your notebook. Then make a list of miracles that have happened in your life—unexpected twists of fate and chance encounters that led to important relationships and opportunities. Think hard about what you set out to do when your miracle occurred. Record all the details: what you thought was going to happen, what actually did happen, where this led you, and any other outcomes you can think of.

You might be surprised to find you've experienced more miracles than you ever thought possible.

why geniuses have genius

AS FAR AS I CAN TELL, true genius is a fairly simple affair. What geniuses do is straightforward enough—they recognize their gifts, and then they fully and completely embrace their craft.

By this I mean that they live it, twenty-four hours a day, for most of their adult life. The stories abound. Rumor has it that the English painter Lucien Freud rarely leaves his London studio, except to visit the National Museum during his favorite off-hours, between 11 P.M. and 5 A.M. To prepare for a role, the actor Daniel Day-Lewis will do things like live in a small box for days to recreate the physical limitations of a character with cerebral palsy. The great soprano Marilyn Horne does not speak while on tour, not even a word, until each night's concert has been given. The painter Andrew Wyeth does not wear a watch, for fear that any sort of schedule will interrupt the flow of his painting.

These people have achieved success because they surrendered fully and completely to their passion. Their first and utmost priority in their life is their work, and they give themselves to it without question. Geniuses do not wake up some days and "just not feel like it"; long ago they passed the threshold where one is controlled by such fleeting thoughts. Their work is the love of their life, a pull they are physically unable to resist. This is how Beethoven composed the Ninth Symphony when he was stone deaf. This is how Monet painted his garden with his paintbrushes strapped to hands crippled with arthritis. This is how Matisse, in the final, most incredible phase of his career, created masterpieces of color and simplicity from his sickbed as an invalid. What the genius knows is out-and-out surrender to creativity.

Once success begins, there is also the issue of responsibility. Geniuses will keep creating on a certain level because it is expected of them. But they also recognize the sacredness of the creative process and so remain authentic to the call. Consider the Nobel Prize–winning Japanese novelist Kenzaburo Oe, who quit writing fiction at the height of his popularity in Japan and around the world. Oe, who in his novels wrote almost exclusively about his brain-damaged son, felt he'd said everything he had to say in his fiction. And so he stopped, with the same bravery and total respect for honesty that had made him a success in the first place.

There are similar stories about the legendary airplane designer Clarence L. "Kelly" Johnson, who founded Lockheed's underground technology think tank, the Skunk Works. In their book *Organizing Genius*, authors Warren Bennis and Patricia Ward Biederman cite one Johnson story in which he returned millions of dollars to the Air Force after deciding his team could not build a hydrogen-powered plane. Johnson did this freely, despite the considerable financial loss such a move meant for Lockheed.

A genius will also surrender to all the emotional demands of his work, no matter how frightening or challenging they may be, even if they entail public excoriation. Orson Welles will always be considered a genius, and *Citizen Kane* will always be one of the great movies of all time, but not because either was polite, well-liked, or properly socialized. In fact, *Citizen Kane* (which was a scathing, thinly-veiled portrayal of William Randolph Hearst and his mistress, Marion Davies) was screened only briefly after it was made and won only one Oscar (for best screenplay). The movie was hidden away in the RKO vault for more than a decade because the studio was afraid to fully release it. And as for Welles, he was openly booed at the 1941 Oscars each time his name was mentioned, and he retained semi-pariah status for the rest of his career. Yet when you look at *Citizen Kane* even today, it is almost overpowering in its freshness. It remains a unique, haunting portrait of a character that, like the best of Shakespeare, simply refuses to go away.

The story is the same throughout history. Look at how impressionism began: Manet, Monet, Renoir, and Degas first showed their vision to the world outside the Academy in Paris, in a tent bearing the sign "Salon des Réfusés" (Exhibit of the Rejects), after Academy officials refused to exhibit their work. Parisian crowds laughed at the paintings and were particularly scandalized by Manet's *Olympia*, a portrait of a common woman, most likely a prostitute, painted utterly realistically to mock the Academy's neoclassical "divine maidens." In fact, *Olympia* had to be hung high, so to be kept safe from the walking sticks and umbrellas people hurled in its direction. Yet today these works are among the most beloved of all paintings, while neoclassicism long ago stopped drawing huge crowds.

Genius is brash and audacious. It smashes convention with delight and refuses to be ignored. It defies the social animal in all of us that's trained to be polite, clever, and adorable, and it chooses the path of raw veracity every time. Genius exists for itself and the sheer joy of its release into the world, and yet it exists for us as well. We need its power and its roughness, just as we need the tranquillity of the everyday.

Geniuses have genius because they simply have no choice. Their gift is prodigious enough that they won't have a moment's peace until they have ridden its wild horses straight into the sun. And all of us, in fact, have a touch of this genius. Whether our gift is baking bread, assessing environmental hazards, teaching children, or powerhouse investing, it's never going to be enough to just dabble a little here and a little there. If you wish for full satisfaction, you must give yourself completely to this work, 100 percent. Now, this does not mean that you have to quit your day job and go live on the street while you pursue your goal. Nor does it mean you must live like a hermit and eschew normality. Rather, when you are able to work, you must dive into your pursuit with bravery, gusto, and out-and-out abandon. And above all else, you must work!

Do not hold back or quibble over details. Do not doubt your process or be afraid. Open the floodgates and let yourself disappear into your vision. Turn yourself inside out and risk complete exposure. Dig into the raw material before you as if it were raw clay craving your touch. No matter what you do, do it as fully and completely as you can. And like so much butterfat, the work which has the highest concentration of "you" will rise to the surface first, crying out to be tasted.

No one has ever celebrated a genius who took things only halfway. Indeed, the world looks to them not just for vision and inspiration but to take comfort in the pure dare of celebrating life as fully as possible.

This is the province of true creative genius, a place of no boundaries, no restraints, and no taboos.

try this...

Visit the local bookstore or library and find some books about geniuses in your field who inspire you. As you read, keep a notebook handy for recording observations that can inform your path. Xerox photographs of your heroes and hang them in your workplace. Or pick some pertinent quotations and use them to create a screen saver for your computer with customizable screen-saver software. Subscribe to a magazine that publishes success stories and information on people who've achieved similar dreams. Keep a file of these news items for easy reference.

when talent does and doesn't matter

THERE SEEMS TO BE ONE PREVAILING BELIEF about talent in our world: either you got it or you don't. And if you don't, you might as well shell peas in the corner of a grocery for the rest of your life.

Well, I, for one, say "phooey."

It may be a fact that some of us lucked out in the gene pool more than others. Talent is a real and undeniable aspect of the success of many great achievers. There is a reason Yo-Yo Ma was at Julliard by the time he was nine. It's no mistake that Bill Gates quit Harvard to invent DOS programming. But let's talk about all the successful people out there who *don't* have extraordinary talent, for in some ways their rise is even more spectacular.

Take Madonna, for instance. Now, Madonna has a fine voice, and she can certainly dance, but one could argue that her superstar status really has to do with more than just her talent. For one thing, the woman is a human dynamo. She has no fear whatsoever about asking for what she wants. Furthermore, she is unafraid to reinvent herself continually to stay fresh and fascinating to her fans. Madonna's genius is in her awareness of what people want and her ability to provide it.

In other words, if you haven't got it, invent it.

We can be fairly sure Madonna never stood around twisting her hair and saying, "If only I could sing like Aretha Franklin." The fact is, Madonna didn't even set out to be a singer. She came to New York to be a dancer, drifted into drumming, and was discovered by two French promoters at Danceteria, a disco that was the epicenter of the New York club scene in the early '80s. "You should sing," they said, and so she did. Several voice lessons later, she got her first major record deal. And as the A&R person who signed her said, she just had that certain something, that superstar quality. Yet that quality wasn't in her voice or her packaging; it was in her presence. Madonna had the ability to sit in a chair and project the essence of a star, which I attribute to two things: crystal-clear vision and a will of steel.

The fact is, you don't have to have talent to be a star, but you absolutely must believe you will become one, come hell or high water. And so, you must also have an indomitable will. Your road will not be easy. You will certainly endure rejection upon rejection. You will have to work harder than you ever thought imaginable. You might even go the route Madonna did in her early days, sleeping in abandoned buildings and eating from garbage cans. Or you could choose the safe route and get a nine-to-five job, but here your will must be even stronger to save you from that cozy, sleepy stupor of security that can undermine creative resolve. At any rate, it won't be easy, and God knows it won't be fair.

Yet, whoever said life was fair to begin with?

Think of all the incredibly talented people out there right now who don't even have enough faith in their abilities to pick up a paintbrush or face a blank spreadsheet. I'd wager there are far more of them than the tiny minority of the less talented whose wonderful audacity keeps pushing them forward. I would also wager there is room in this world for both, so ultimately, talent is not even an issue.

However, since this is an imperfect world, talent occasionally is an issue. Say you want to be a singer. If you really don't have a perfect "instrument," as the voice teachers call it, you will face frustration, and it will be commensurate with the size of your dream. If you want to be Madonna, you have to at least be able to carry a tune, feel the beat, and sound pretty musical. And you have to be willing to work your tail off to make not only your voice but your entire persona into something salable. You have to be willing to do whatever it takes to make your dream happen. And ultimately, and perhaps most importantly, you have to be willing to fail.

You have to love yourself so much that, even after years of vocal coaching, dance lessons, head shots, costume fittings, demo tapes, videos, practice gigs, mailing lists, cold calls, business letters, auditions, rejections, constant practicing, and the endless grind of just trying to find an audience, you can walk away quietly when the time comes, knowing you did what you had to do. If it doesn't work out, you'll have to be able to make your peace with your inability to become the next Madonna. And perhaps, in doing so, see that following your dream really wasn't all about the satisfaction of your ego and whether or not you went on worldwide tours attracting millions of fans. What it was really about was the nourishment of your own fantastic spirit. You gave yourself a profound gift, and that you didn't "succeed" was not even entirely true, for you may have even discovered that great universal secret: *the doing of the work is where true pleasure lies.*

You will have grown in subtle and important ways, and so you will hopefully scan the horizon for the next dream you can appropriate, the next adventure you can set off on. In this way, you can never lose; you can only grow, through perseverance, sweat, and the happy broadcast of your own fantastic dreams.

try this...

Test your will by checking off the statements that apply to you:

There are things I want to do in life, and I'll get to them—in my nineties.

If given a choice between putting some time in on my business idea and rotating my tires, I'll go with the tires every time.

I'd probably write the great American novel if I didn't have a television.

I can no longer open the guest-room closet because it's full of all the craft projects I started but never finished.

I'd like to do something creative, but I haven't got a creative bone in my body.

I definitely had more will when I was younger.

I could do a better job than any of the so-called super-stars in my field. I just don't feel like it.

If you checked any of the above, chances are you need to reexamine where you stand with your will. Take a minute and complete the following lists. Feel free to be brutally honest.

What I'm Afraid of Finding Out about My Dream
What It Will Mean If I Succeed at My Dream
What Will Change If I Succeed at My Dream
People Who Support My Dream
People Who Do Not Support My Dream
What I Will Gain By Pursuing My Dream

read this in case
of emergency

UNLIKE THE REST OF LIFE, an emergency in your creative process is inevitable. In other words, if you set off on the long road to realizing your vision, you can expect some major traffic jams ahead.

This does not mean you have to get off the road altogether.

It simply means that great things are seldom created without some breakdowns along the way.

Why is this? you might ask. I contend it is because we are only human beings—and pretty limited ones at that. We're insatiable when it comes to praise, accomplishment, and looking good. And we're pretty damn pitiful when it comes to hanging with something for the long haul and having a little faith. Bottom line: We enter most creative enterprises from the mind-set of "I'll try it, but my results had better be brilliant *now*—or else."

This is sort of like trying to master origami in an afternoon; it's simply not going to happen, no matter how hard we try. And not only that, by rushing the process we never get to experience the thrill of gradual mastery.

Something almost chemical happens when you try, try, and try, only to master something after long and committed effort. The voices of doubt are thrown into happy submission, and for at least ten minutes you can actually be a hero in your own mind. Enough of these small triumphs and you might even accumulate some serious self-esteem. It's a slow win, but it's a real one, the rewards of which are yours forever.

In the meanwhile, you will inevitably bog down. It may be that your project gets off to a fantastic start. You're clear-headed, inspired, full of ideas, and tear home from work each night, eager to get to it. That's the first week, or the first month, even. Then you have a bad day. The boss calls you names. Your computer crashes. The promised promotion goes to someone else. You limp home, licking your wounds, and instead of turning to your project for a bit of soul healing, you crack open a beer and turn on the news. "I've had a helluva day," you justify. "Don't I deserve a night off?"

What gets forgotten at such a moment is the power your work has to restore your wounded spirit. "Give me a break," you sigh. Well, OK—we all *do* deserve a night off once in a while. But the disaster happens the next night, when you consider how easy it was to slough off your project the night before. "Still recovering," you murmur to yourself as you head off to happy hour. Two months later, there's a half inch of dust on the work that was originally intended to save your life. Years later, you still have a dim memory of that book you were going to write, and it's soaked in resignation and regret.

When we feel like quitting, we confuse concentrated effort with back-breaking labor. The view from the downy, soft contours of our overstuffed armchairs is definitely stilted. Indeed, it seems virtually impossible to get up and make phone calls, create financial projections, test recipes, or do anything. *I can't, I just can't. I'm too tired. I'm too weak. I can't even think straight. I just worked all day! How can I possibly create?* At that moment, it seems the effort is just plain more than we can bear.

There are always going to be moments in your process when you think yourself straight to hell. You're going to be convinced you're too tired, too uninspired, or too depressed. A million other temptations will beckon. The mere idea of sitting at your desk will seem impossible until you actually sit down and do it. Thinking about it is what will immobilize you—just thinking about it. The actual work, if you can get yourself to begin, will probably be relatively easy.

Alex Forbes, a friend of mine who is a professional singer/songwriter, calls this "The Wall." In the course of nearly every song she writes, she hits a place where she just can't go on. Any spark of inspiration in what she'd already written has somehow died, and finishing the song now seems impossible. And yet, she knows she cannot just walk away and not return. So Alex sits there, noodling around, waiting for something to happen, trying not to despair.

All of us hit The Wall sooner or later, yet it can be a place of great reward. Alex has found that if she can just hang in there and press through her resistance, a breakthrough usually lies on the other side: an incredible bridge section that lifts the song to a whole new place, or a lyric that really gets at the heart of the matter. Every so often, however, The Wall wins. When this happens, Alex is forced to confront the fact that the song she's trying to write is really just a piece of useless fluff that doesn't deserve song status. In these cases, what The Wall demands is some serious soul-searching and truth-telling. Alex has come to realize that not every creative impulse needs to be pursued to completion. She now sees The Wall as a productive and important part of her own process.

Yet, here you are, still sitting in your comfy armchair. And the work is still sitting on your desk, staring you in the face. So it is simply a matter of picking yourself out of the armchair, *even when you don't feel like doing it*, and getting to it. It's been proven again and again: all you have to do is do it. Soon enough, the creative process will draw you in once again, warming you, enriching you, soothing all your dark defenses, welcoming you back home.

It's simply a matter of staying on the truest course.

try this...

The next time you need to work on your project but "just don't feel like it," give yourself the gift of a few minutes to consider why.

Perhaps these questions will help. Answer honestly— they're for you.

1. What would you rather be doing right now?

2. If you were doing that other thing, how much would your life actually improve?

3. What's the bottom-line truth about why you are avoiding your project?

4. What are you afraid of?

5. How will you feel if you don't go back to work?

6. How will you feel if you do?

how false modesty
kills dreams

RECENTLY, ON THE *TODAY* SHOW, I saw a boy named Paris Goudi, not more than twelve years old, who was skillfully juggling balls in front of an impromptu street audience. The host, in her best coifed-for-the-camera manner, gave him a gratuitous smile and asked, "Gee, aren't you nervous juggling on national television?"

The boy's eyes never strayed from his efforts—five balls that he was now juggling behind his head. "Nope," he said simply. "This is my home. This is where I belong."

Amen.

We should all be so supremely confident that we can say the unthinkable before an audience of 3.5 million. And this was the unthinkable. This kid did not have some megawatt agent wrangling him a spot on national television. Chances are he didn't have a PR person or even a manager. The network's crew just happened to bump into him on a sidewalk in New York, but then, Paris Goudi already knew that national television was his home. And more importantly, he put that information into his speaking.

There has been much said about the power of our speech. In her excellent book, *Jesus, CEO*, which examines Jesus as the extraordinary leader that he was, Laurie Beth Jones notes that Jesus never denigrated himself in language. Rather, in Isaiah 55:11, he said, "I declare a thing and it is done for me. My word accomplishes that which I send it out to do." This is not conceit; it is a simple statement of fact. Our words are our messengers. And it wasn't just Jesus who could make this happen. So it is with all our words—we really are what we speak. *Really.*

In leading my workshops, I often hear people present work to the group by beginning with a preamble: "This probably stinks, but..." "I know this isn't any good, but..." "I tried, but this was the best I could do..." I like to think of this weird human reflex as the Parade of False Modesty. It's an automatic urge to publicly denigrate anything you've created—whether you secretly think it's good or not—in order to save face should the thing bomb. And whenever the Parade of False Modesty begins, I find myself taking a major step back in interest. It's as if these people are actively willing me not to like their work, no matter how wonderful it is.

What the Parade of False Modesty does is immediately snatch a little joy from the intended audience, and for what effect? Just so that person can avoid the squirming vulnerability which comes with true self-expression. Just so he or she can squeeze into the paradigm of cool for a moment, because, let's admit it, these days self-confident is not a totally hip way to be. It's only a self-loving way to be, which in our ironic age almost never flies.

You will never achieve what you set out to do unless you can get squarely behind it, believe in its power, and actively speak that belief. You will never make anything happen if you have to keep hiding behind false modesty. And you must remember that while this work comes from you, it is not yours alone to kick, punch, and mutilate at will. In fact, your work belongs to the rest of us as well.

This is why you have to watch your speaking, for if you constantly insist that your work is inadequate, your life is inadequate, or you are inadequate, the world will respond accordingly. Rather than seeing you as the hip, witty, urbane individual you hope to be, we will hear your denigrating words and take that deadly step backward. We will feel robbed, and rightly so, of the chance to see you and your work for themselves. And since we will smell a self-made loser, rather than pay serious attention, we will simply pass you by.

The same is also true of the reverse. People who have the self-respect to speak kindly of themselves and their processes are usually rewarded with success. Walt Whitman not only self-published the initial editions of *Leaves of Grass*, he also wrote his own reviews, describing himself as "large and lusty, a naive, masculine, affectionate, contemplative, sensual, imperious person." Not unlike Paris Goudi, Whitman knew he belonged in the public eye and had no problem saying so. And so, rather than bragging, he simply stated a fact. And in doing so, he introduced himself to us as a person whose gifts we all might share.

When you step forth and express yourself, your audience hears one thing: how generous a gift you are willing to give. Think for a moment about your own speaking. Are you in the "Oh, it's really nothing, just a little something I scratched out, it's probably terrible" camp, or are you more like Paris? When someone compliments your work, do you immediately jump down their throat with a list of its imperfections? Or do you say thank you and allow their appreciation to sink in for a moment? Giving others the chance to appreciate you is, in fact, another way of giving back to them. It completes the cycle that all this giving generated in the first place, which is what your loving audience demands.

So what this all boils down to ultimately is your sense of generosity. Can you actually bring yourself to clothe your dreams in the respect and love that they deserve? They are your children, in a sense. So, can you speak of them as the powerful, wonderful creations that they are? Or do you defeat them with your words so that they, like you, stay small and limited?

Will you give the gift or not? While the answer may ultimately lie in your actions, it truly does begin in your words.

Take a look and see. Are your words delivering the message that you want?

try this...

Unplug the phone; kick out kids, spouse, and neighbors; and give yourself some peace and quiet. Then get a large pad of paper, several pencils or pens, and a very comfortable chair. Pour a little tea, if you like, and put on some undistracting, soothing music. Then make a grand, master list of all the beliefs that keep you from moving forward with your project.

Here are some limiting beliefs that have come up in my workshops: "I'm not qualified." "I have to do this every day or not at all!" "I'll offend too many people." "My mother will never forgive me." Press through the voice in your head that's trying to distract you, and be relentless with yourself. *Keep going until you have revealed at least twenty-five limiting beliefs.*

proof that rejection
won't kill you

THE FIRST TIME I EVER WROTE A NOVEL, there was a monotonous hum in the background the entire time. It was my mind chanting, "The first time this gets rejected I will die. The first time this gets rejected I will die."

Somehow I managed to finish the thing and put it into the hands of a few people I knew in the publishing business. The first rejection rolled in from the sister of a friend, a six-month publishing novice who was a secretary to a famous editor. "Well, first of all," she began, "the whole thing needs a major haircut."

A haircut! A HAIRCUT!! sputtered my indignant mind. *Why don't we just shave it all off and go bald?* "Hmm," I said, as noncommittally as I could.

"Yes, and some of these characters, Suzanne..." her voice trailed off in dismay. "How shall I put this? They were just...well...trite."

Trite? TRITE???!!! Now my mind was under siege and there was emergency help running in from all directions. Somehow, and I don't remember how, I managed to wind up the conversation and get off the phone before she finished her critique, whereupon I broke down into racking, heaving sobs. My book had been soundly rejected—hated, even.

Yet I did not die.

Ultimately, I signed with a literary agent who did his best to sell the book, but no one wanted to buy it. Every couple of weeks or so for an entire year, another elegant, cream-colored rejection letter with my name neatly typed on it would slip through the mail slot. For a while, they just accumulated on my desk, but then one day I shored up my soul and sat down and read them one by one, all twenty-seven of them. Immediately, I began to understand something about rejection: *it's nothing personal.*

Seriously.

In fact, almost every rejection letter gave a different reason for not buying my book. Some editors wanted the book but couldn't convince their bosses or their marketing teams to buy it. Others loved the writing but not the plot. Some didn't like the characters or the fact that the book didn't have a stronger social relevance. But not one of them said a word about me, personally. No letter said, "How can you send me a book by such a loser?" or "What kind of idiot wrote this thing?"—all of which seemed entirely possible to my warped thinking. The bottom line was that my book had been rejected by every single publisher in New York, but not only did I survive, I managed to keep on writing.

What I learned from this experience was nonattachment. This is quite literally the difference between those who achieve their dream and those who don't.

For every person who cannot put their dream in place, there is a whole lot of silent screaming going on: *Help! I might finish it. Help! It might succeed. Help! I might finally be someone and have to answer for myself in the world. Help! Recognition will probably destroy me.* The sad thing is, it isn't us the world is waiting to recognize; it is only our work. This is where nonattachment comes in.

First and foremost, *we are not our work.* We are living, breathing people who create businesses, artworks, ideas, and babies. But these are not, and never will be, us. Still, somehow, in the process of caring a hell of a lot about something and pouring all your sweat and blood into it, you can get terribly confused.

When a performer goes out on stage, they may feel that the audience is judging every aspect of them and their life. In fact, all that poor audience is doing is waiting to be entertained a little. They aren't commenting on the actor's looks, politics, hairstyle, or intelligence. These things are really the farthest thing from their minds. When they applaud, they are just telling the performer that they liked what she did at that particular moment, in that particular place. That's all. The rest, quite honestly, they don't even care about, nor should they be expected to.

So it isn't up to me what the world thinks of me; the world will think what it thinks, and I have no control over this. Indeed, my job is simply to do the work and send it out there. That is all—end of story. It isn't up to me to make the world like me, any more than it is up to me to determine the fate of my creative undertakings. In fact, I contend that the more honest, provocative, and truly vulnerable I am with my work, the more vocal will be those who despise it. However, by the same token, my honesty will genuinely touch even more people as well.

What we have to keep remembering is to release these gifts as easily and as effortlessly as they were given to us in the first place. We must release these gifts, not because they will make us rich or because they bear any significance at all, but simply because they flowed through us and must now be given away—either to the public at large or even just to someone we love. And should we decide to go public with the work and it gets rejected once or even hundreds of times, we simply need to follow our instincts and keep on releasing it until we sense it is time to stop. Perhaps our work will be appreciated; perhaps it won't. What is critical is that we created it in the first place and so have grown in the process.

Each project we undertake is merely another milestone on our own particular path, a signpost that has to be passed in order to reach the next one. We all have our share of scathing reviews, bitter rejections, and out-and-out failures, but ultimately, who even cares? The bigger question is, can you go to bed comforted by the thought that you came a little closer toward accomplishing your vision? Can you say to yourself, I did my work—my real work—today?

Creativity is a selfless act, demanding that you give of yourself simply for the sheer love of giving. We cannot give our work to the world expecting anything in return at all. That this simple act requires courage is merely creativity's gift back to us.

try this...

Take a moment and assess: How exactly do you handle rejection? Are you a quitter? A pouter? A take-it-on-the-chin type? Someone who seeks revenge? Or do you avoid rejection altogether by never starting anything in the first place?

If you're not sure, try writing down at least three times you suffered rejection (work-related or personal). Then carefully reconstruct exactly how you handled each experience. What is the status of those efforts today? Was anything learned?

when to run, not walk, from helpful advice

THERE ARE PEOPLE OUT THERE who would like to see you realize your dreams, and there are people who would not. These so-called friends come in all guises—family, co-workers, even teachers. For whatever reason, they relish defeat and take comfort in helping plant the seed of your defeat as well.

Avoid them at all costs.

Once you have begun the pursuit of your vision in earnest, you will be tempted to share it with the world. This may be news of your very first sale as a realtor, or some early bottles of wine from your own small vineyard, or the manuscript of your first novel. You lug all 2,500 pages of it into your office, drop it at the feet of that guy across the hall who kept saying you never could do it, and stand back to enjoy a moment of smug satisfaction.

"There," you say with a smile. "Want to read it?"

The guy across the hall is the wrong person to show your precious work to at this moment, for he is not, and never will be, your ally. And no matter how victorious you may feel at the huge progress you've made, your creative self is still painfully fragile. All this so-called friend has to do is shove it with his toe and say, "Yeah, sure . . . when I've got some time," and suddenly your dream deflates a tiny bit.

And then, God forbid he does get some time. He'll return the manuscript, saying only, "Pretty good—I mean, I didn't believe a word of it and I thought the plot was pretty dismal, but hey, what do I know?" Chances are the manuscript will find its way to a dark corner under your desk, where it will sit collecting dust, far into the future.

It is my belief that the only people truly qualified to give opinions of your work are the professionals directly involved—the investors, dealers, agents, critics, publishers, managers, directors, producers, admissions boards, licensing bureaus, and bureaucratic chiefs—in other words, people who get paid for their opinions. Everyone else will have an opinion, of course, but this by no means implies that you should listen to it.

Still, we are gluttons for punishment. In some sick way we *want* the guy across the hall to hate it so the ever-chiming voice of doubt can be right for once. Then we're off the hook! No one else has to ever see the work! All the hard work, risk, and discomfort is over! Blissfully, we can sink back into our armchair and assume permanent couch-potato position and just forget the whole damn dream business that started all this in the first place. So we're defeated, we smirk, reaching for a fistful of chips. Who gives a damn? At least we can relax for a change.

As you and I both know, it ain't that simple.

The guy across the hall hates our book, and so we've just died a thousand small deaths. And yet, the phoenix can and will rise from the ashes, as we proceed to do what we should have done in the first place. We go to the library and research agents, managers, licensing bureaus, or whoever the gatekeeper is for our chosen field. We locate books and professional organizations where we can find information on how best to approach these folks, learning whatever etiquette may be required. We get the education we need to make the mark, and we join clubs or enroll in classes that help us learn how to market our efforts. We network, calling everyone we ever knew, asking if they happen to know anyone who might be helpful. And then, and only then, do we pass our creation on to maybe one or two trusted, true friends, *the kind who honestly want to see us succeed.* (You know who these people are, and if you don't, start looking for them. Everyone needs at least one ally.)

Our supporters will have ideas for us, and many of them may be of value. If they happen to be proficient in our chosen field, then all the better. But remember one thing: they are not, and never should become, our gods. Treat their opinions as nothing more than what they are—opinions.

My father, John Falter, was an artist who as a very young child exhibited a natural talent for draftsmanship. When he was fifteen, his parents took him to the nearest big city and showed samples of cartoons he'd been publishing in the local paper to a successful syndicated cartoonist there. "This boy will never be a great cartoonist," the man decreed. "He draws too well." My father so revered this man's opinion that he basically wrote off cartoon work for the rest of his life.

Even though he became one of the most important illustrators of his generation, a small part of him always longed to do cartoons. A number of times over the years, he submitted cover ideas to *The New Yorker*, each with legitimately funny concepts, but they were always turned down. Perhaps the cartoonist was right, but maybe he wasn't. What's certain is that my father never felt confident as a cartoonist after this prediction, despite his success as an artist. He never published a cartoon again.

Mentors and teachers need to be treated with a degree of caution as well. Far too often they teach not to inspire and encourage their students into working but to snag a precious audience and feed their ravenous egos. Beware of teachers who make denigration a key factor of teaching. Constructive criticism should never be confused with public humiliation. In fact, criticism cannot even be heard by a student unless it is delivered in a gentle, soul-informing way: a way that acknowledges the student's own innate gifts.

Also, beware of classes where the teacher sits back and turns the students into teachers. These free-for-alls can turn into slash-and-burn sessions that are more about competition than anything else. I remember an advertising copywriting class I took once, taught by an award-winning creative director, in which the students (90 percent of whom had never worked in advertising) were challenged to "find the holes" in each other's work. By mid-semester, 50 percent of the class had stopped coming. By the end, only three of us remained. It is safe to say a whole lot of learning did not go on there.

I think the fact is that we are far more fragile than we think. True self-expression demands incredible vulnerability, and so we must treat our work as the precious gift that it is. The urge to share may be wonderful and irrepressible, but we need to be smart about it. For this is not ours, this thing we have created; it's divine work that has been put in our hands, however briefly. To be careful stewards, we must proceed with open eyes, fully cognizant of the minefield ahead. Only then will our work find the souls it was intended to touch, and only then will our job be complete.

try this...

Begin a file and fill it with the encouraging notes, e-mails, and letters you collect along your path. These could be messages from supporters, parents, kids, colleagues, and professionals—anyone who was genuinely touched by what you're doing and wants to support your efforts. The file can even include rejection letters from people who see and state the value of your work. Feel free to plunge in and read them whenever your morale needs a boost.

in praise of failure

ONE REASON MANY PEOPLE NEVER GET AROUND to pursuing their dream is what psychologists and other analytical types call "fear of failure." Essentially, one is so paralyzed by the mere possibility that they might fail that they do backflips to avoid such a catastrophe. Well, to any of you who might be feeling this way, I have only a few choice words: get over it already.

Not only is failure an essential and important part of your progress, it is unavoidable. No matter what you set out to do, sooner or later there will be a failure, whether it is a complete and total belly flop at the onset that redirects your course, or a later one, after you've become an established success. Basically, experiencing failure is like arguing with a spouse—nobody wants to do it, but sooner or later it's bound to happen. And handled intelligently, failure won't be a disaster at all. Rather, it will yield all sorts of important information about your well-being and your conduct in life.

While it may seem a gross generalization to say that nobody can avoid failure, when you think about it, it's true. More often than not, failure is simply the smashing of our expectations. It is the rerouting of our vision onto a different course. And while we hardly like the experience, it is wonderful in a way, because it shakes us from our smugness. It reminds us how little we actually know about this path that we're on. It pulls us back up to the job of reinventing ourselves, returning us to the essential work of creation. If our egos will just let us get on with it, failure calls us forward once again as creators.

There is a wonderful story about Stephen Crane. His novel *Maggie: A Girl of the Streets* was found to be too realistic and grim for commercial publishing of the 1890s. So, unable to find a publisher, the author published it himself, only to sell one hundred copies. Unfortunately, Crane had spent his entire savings on the book, so he was forced to burn the remainders for fuel. However, one of the few copies that was left reached William Dean Howells. It was Howells who helped to get Crane's classic *The Red Badge of Courage* published subsequently. Afterward, *Maggie* was republished to roaring success.

Michael Klepper and Robert Gunther's book, *The Wealthy 100*, tells the story about one of the wealthiest men in U.S. history, Cyrus H. McCormick. McCormick, a farmer's son, dedicated his entire adult life to the development of a horse-drawn reaping machine, a project his father had begun. After several years of refinement, he finally got the design right. Then he spent nine years trying to convince farmers, who had been harvesting their fields by hand with scythes, that his invention actually worked. There were no buyers. The panic of 1837 followed and McCormick went bankrupt; the bank repossessed everything except his reaper, which they decided wasn't worth a dime—which was fortunate, since McCormick was not about to give up.

After two more years of doggedly dragging farmers out into fields and demonstrating his machine, he finally sold one. Four years later, he'd sold fifty of them. He tried everything to market his invention—money-back guarantees, payment plans, and testimonial advertising, which was unheard of then. Six years later, he'd sold three thousand reapers. Then he demonstrated the machine in Europe, and before a skeptical crowd, he harvested seventy-four yards of wheat in seventy seconds. After a moment of stunned silence, the crowd began to cheer wildly. McCormick took home international medals and the applause of the press. By the time of his death, thirty-three years later, McCormick's reaping machine had amassed a fortune of ten million dollars and launched a company known today as International Harvester.

The story of Michelangelo at San Lorenzo is similar. Michelangelo—who was thrown out of the house as an infant, raised by a wet nurse, and beaten by his father for wanting to be an artist—began working on the church at San Lorenzo after establishing himself as Italy's preeminent monumental sculptor. As William Wallace relates in his fine biography, *Michelangelo at San Lorenzo*, Michelangelo was originally to design and sculpt all the statuary on the church facade. After two months of working with the architect, however, he decided that only he could design a building magnificent enough for his sculpture. (Michelangelo had never before designed a building.) He won the commission, and thinking big as usual, declared that he would "domesticate the mountains" and create "the mirror of architecture and sculpture of all Italy."

What Michelangelo set out to do was create a facade for the church that would include twenty enormous columns, each made from a massive piece of marble. Each piece would have to be hauled by horse-drawn sledge, cart, boat, and finally on foot, from the other end of Italy. (This was long before dynamite and heavy trucks with transmissions were invented.) Four years later, Michelangelo had opened a new quarry, built roads to it, designed a massive crane for hauling the marble, devised a pinion system for moving the loads around steep, twisting mountaintop roads, and employed an entire army of three hundred quarry men and stone movers.

Michelangelo personally spent more than eight months just checking out veins of marble. He was nearly killed when one of the columns, because of a faulty iron ring, smashed to the ground as it was being lifted out of the quarry. And this was only one of seven columns he quarried—five more disappeared en route. Only one column actually made it to San Lorenzo, where it still lies today, covered with moss in a ditch near the church.

Later that year, the pope who commissioned the work died, Michelangelo's contract was terminated, and the project was given to other designers to complete more simply. Michelangelo wrote to the Vatican, "I am not charging to this account the fact that I have been ruined over the said work at San Lorenzo;

I am not charging to this account the enormous insult of having been brought here to execute the said work, and then having it taken away from me. . . . I am left with two handfuls of toil and a striving after wind."

When he wrote this, Michelangelo did not know that he would go on to spend the last third of his career as one of the world's great architects or that the facade of San Lorenzo would always remain unfinished out of respect for what he began. All he knew was that he'd tried architecture and failed miserably. Yet the architectural triumph of the Medici Chapel still awaited him, as did St. Peter's. At this moment, Michelangelo's sense of failure was the same as anyone's. It seemed like a hopeless situation from which nothing good could ever be derived.

History has proven, however, that his failure was anything but complete. Indeed, the facade for San Lorenzo took him into an entirely new era in his career. So, like all failures, it was simply a rearrangement of plans, a sudden and unexpected blow to one's expectations.

Most failure is not an end in itself but a beginning disguised as an end. The only true failure would have been for Michelangelo to stop caring and stick his sculpture into a facade he considered unworthy. The only true failure would have been for him to arrest that part of himself which refused to acquiesce. That would have been the death of his vision and a strike against his almost unbearable passion, an emotional force so powerful the townspeople gave it a name: Michelangelo's *terribilita*.

So there really is no such thing as failure. There is only the rearrangement of plans and the surrender of ego. There is only the twist in the road we never expect. As long as we remain true to our vision and ourselves, we simply cannot fail. That is all we have to remember.

try this...

Make a list of the ten most important failures in your life and what they led to. Were they true failures, or were they simply a rearrangement of your plans? What was learned or gained? Have you forgiven yourself yet?

the benefits of wishing for too much

AS A NATION, WE ARE CONSTIPATED WISHERS. And who can blame us? Most of us grew up in homes where epithets like "Be careful what you wish for. You just might get it!" were constantly being hurled in our faces.

Be careful what you wish for. You just might get it. What exactly does this mean, anyway?

I interpret it to mean, Don't bother to consciously desire happiness, challenge, and growth, because you, oh worthless one, couldn't begin to handle it.

I also interpret it to mean that we are doomed to a life of fruitless wishing for fruitless pursuits that would probably be so stressful (even if they did come true, which they won't) they'd end up killing us.

Well, excuse me for living.

I, personally, am a passionate believer in wishing, and I think we should all do far more of it. And yet, there is a definite art to it, which I have learned from not only the occasional wish come true but from a thousand or so wishes that have been dashed.

The magic is this: My wishes never work when I don't really believe I deserve them.

An example. From time to time, in a casual, backhanded sort of way, I've wished for a million dollars. It's a Pavlovian response, an automatic answer when the subject of wishing comes up. Sure, I'd love a million dollars. Who wouldn't? But in the very next second, I also inevitably have the thought that

I'll never get it. A million dollars just doesn't fit in my radar screen. It's too vast a sum, too huge a gift. It doesn't seem possible, not given the little person I really, actually, secretly am. And so my wish dries up and blows away, another fruitless thought.

The truth is, I could never accept a million dollars unless I believed I'd done something spectacular enough to merit it. So, when I look at it, I don't really want the cartoon suitcase bulging with bills. What I want is work that's worth a million dollars to the world. Then my wish feels stronger, more plausible, truly worth wishing for. It seems like something I might even deserve.

Recently I was looking through the paper and saw an ad for a one-night-only benefit performance of unpublished songs by the late Jonathan Larson, the creator of *Rent*. I am a huge *Rent* fan and immediately thought to myself that I had to see it. Then I noticed the cost of tickets: $150. Without further ado, I turned the page, but the wish had already been made. I'd connected with my deep desire to go. I didn't question that I deserved to be there. I could even see myself walking into the theater, ready to soak up every last exhilarating ounce of it. I'd thrown it out only because of simple financial logistics, so as far as I knew, I wasn't going. The matter was promptly forgotten.

Three days later, on the afternoon of the performance, a friend called me, offering me a free ticket to see the show. We had orchestra seats that night, and I learned once again the power of deep desire. I was merely adding proof to the fact that you really do get what you want in life.

When my wishes haven't worked out, it's because they came from my stomach instead of my heart. Actually, I really have no idea what part of my body the wishes came from, but they felt like stomach wishes, because they were so incredibly gluttonous. For instance, when I published my first novel, my wishes had me lounging on David Letterman's couch, languidly tossing out bon mots while millions watched and adored. My wishes had me lunching with Sting, turning down screenplay offers left and right, and raking in major literary awards, not to mention escaping from my horribly crowded book signings through a back door to my waiting limo.

The reality of publication included a handful of tiny write-ups in tiny newspapers, book signings where I read to three people I was related to, and a book that almost immediately went out of print. So much for wishing from your stomach.

What I learned was that these wishes were all about me! me! me! and not about them! them! them! It took me several years to get it; at the end of the day, the point of publishing a novel was actually not so I could have my fifteen minutes in the public glare but so I could offer my readers something they might find moving. It was to give my readers a gift.

My wishes have since changed accordingly. I'm learning that wishing for success is not enough. For me to be authentic and feel deserving, my wishes have to be linked to how they serve people. So going on Letterman becomes not about delivering bon mots but about reaching readers so I can share my books with them and do the work I'm supposed to be doing. The wishes are actually as organic to the process as the work itself, and that is why they pertain to you.

In setting out to do our work, we have to constantly keep reminding ourselves that we're in the business of giving gifts. And in order to give these gifts to those who they are intended for, we have to get them out in the world. Wishes help this process, because they force us to focus on exactly what we want to have happen. And while we ultimately have little control, we do have our wishes. If they come from the heart and not the stomach, and if we truly know we deserve them, then big things can and do happen.

Which brings us around to the title of this chapter. Say you spent your vacation shooting color pictures of turtles in the Galapagos, and they're really great. They are by far the best thing you've ever shot, even though you've been nursing your amateur photography habit for years. Everyone who sees them is struck by their power, and all around you the feedback is positive. So what do you do with them?

Your secret wish is that *National Geographic* will buy them, but of course you know this is completely unrealistic. (*Not a chance in hell! Forget about it! I shot these on my vacation, for God's sake!*) On the other hand, your brother-in-law the dentist said he'd buy the lot for $25 and hang them in his waiting room. And someone knows someone at the local newspaper, who might run one extremely small in black-and-white. So you figure that's about as good as it's going to get, and you plod off to the local paper, negatives in hand. Right?

Wrong, wrong, wrong.

Instead of leaping to the chintziest possible conclusions, try sitting there for a while and thinking about where this work really needs to go. Try to connect with the tiny, hopeful shred of self that's still in there, desperately trying to make contact. Forget about your ego for once, and also forget about feeding the gluttonous maw of your self-defeat. And while you're at it, try to cut through any overinflated stomach wishes that may have you feeling a bit bloated. If you can, let yourself really, truly wish for something as deeply as you ever have, something that is of real importance to you.

It's a frightening prospect, getting what you want. Even more frightening is letting yourself believe that you deserve it. Yet this is what separates the people who achieve their dreams from the rest of us. Their passion is so strong for their vision that they are naturally audacious about it. It never occurs to them to wonder whether they're good enough to sell their pictures to *National Geographic*. These people just naturally think big, so they're more concerned with getting the right pictures in the right places. For them, deserving success isn't even a conversation.

So the same can be true for you, but again, only if you think you deserve it. Listen to your instincts about where your work needs to go and who it needs to reach. Perhaps the audience for it will be small and select. On the other hand, perhaps it will sweep the nation.

Be a good mother to your work, and have high hopes for it. Not only do you deserve it, but so do those the work is intended to reach.

By all means, wish for too much. The results may truly astound you.

try this...

Buy yourself a special blank notebook, one you really like. Personalize it by sticking a favorite image on it or writing some key quotations or notes in a visible place on the cover or inside. Then take your notebook to a favorite place: a hammock, a coffee bar, a beach, a park, any place where you really resonate.

Start writing down your wishes in your book—the really true ones you haven't given yourself much time to acknowledge. Let them flow however they do, in lists, words, or even as detailed scenarios. Try not to judge them or get into how you'll implement them. Instead, just let them pour out of you, one after another. Make a regular habit of connecting with your wishes, and when they materialize, make a note of that in your book as well.

why power is more than a trip

THERE IS ONE UGLY QUESTION that really drives this book. It's a simple question, yet for some reason it's one that no one ever wants to hear.

How big are you willing to be?

Not how big are you going to be, but how big are you willing to be, emphasis on the word *willing*.

The power with which you waltz through this life is absolutely and completely in your own hands, and it can be tremendous. Your mind can access infinite wisdom and prosperity, and your body can produce extraordinary health and strength. They will do this for you, but only if you are willing.

If you aren't, what you get is what many of us have: substantial debt, bad backs, annoying children, excruciating jobs. And with that comes a passel of longing for other people's homes, lawns, jobs, lives, kids, and credit ratings. In this country, especially, we believe in the power of more money to lubricate the wounds. We see a larger house as the panacea to a stultifying marriage. We imagine a big vacation to be the thing that will finally bond our families. Yet all of those problems are quite solvable within the confines of our too-small, inadequate homes behind lawns crawling with crabgrass. All it requires is for us to give up being small and whiney, and finally to start to get big.

The process begins with a question: What is it that you get from your current arrangement? And believe me, you're definitely getting something. Inadequate jobs are excellent places to hide. Lousy marriages are wonderful protectors of the soft part of your heart. (God forbid that you are actually with someone who means something to you—you might get hurt!) And having no money relieves one of all those nasty adult responsibilities, like paying taxes, investing in IRAs, and saving for college tuitions.

The mind is wonderfully literate this way, for it truly will produce whatever it is that you want, and by this I don't mean surface desires but those which dwell in that deep place far within. Here is the seat of your power, a place accessed by visualizations, prayers, mantras, dreams, and the subconscious. And while I do not know exactly where this big black place is, I know when I'm in touch with it.

Then my desires run as clear and unimpeded as water in a stream. They're not weighted down with the freight of a million doubting thoughts. They're not scrambling over a mountain of mental logistics. They simply are. *I want to lead workshops. I want to write novels. I want to have a wonderful marriage. I want a son and a daughter.* They are simple moments of truth that we take posession of, know in our soul, and don't let go of, no matter what. And they are forces that drive us through thick and thin and past obstacle after obstacle. They are, in fact, that still, small voice that never, ever gives up.

So why aren't we all walking about like the studly bastions of power we actually are?

Simple. We don't think we're worth it.

We stick ourselves in so-so jobs because this is all we assume we can handle. We believe the ho-hum salary that goes along with it is all we deserve. Like anorexics, we refuse to allow ourselves more than just barely enough money, or health, or love, or sex, or creativity because deep down inside we are ashamed. We figure we are guilty of a thousand unmentionable sins, so why even bother trying to emerge?

Furthermore, we are afraid. Our power is like a huge and unnatural tool to us—a roaring chainsaw, when we're accustomed to using a nail file. Yet the things that chainsaw can and will do for us are amazing when applied with care and precision. All that is required is that we wake up, open our eyes, and start taking responsibility.

We must allow ourselves to actually see what is in front of us and not merely ride along on the old, popular interpretation. We have to listen to what people say around us, putting our concentration into what's coming out of their mouths instead of what's about to come out of ours. We must constantly assess and evaluate from a place of deeper clarity, a place unaware of politics, favors, trends, or the ephemeral workings of coolness. It's those old first-grade rules for crossing the street: Stop, Look, and Listen. All of these are things we were designed to do.

Our power also demands that we act deliberately, for it has no time for sidestepping. We must be unafraid to be utterly honest, to honor our gut feelings on things, and to say and do the unpopular when necessary. We have to give up our addiction to other people's opinions and surrender to the freedom of acting with strength and courage. There will be detractors, just like there always have been. That won't change. What does change when you start to live from your power is that you care progressively less and less.

You will start to see the humor in all their petty concerns. You will actually begin to delight in people's taunting names for you or in the lacerations of the press. Then it will all be so relative it will be scary, because along with power comes massive amounts of perspective and commitment. Another person's snipes and snideness will become a sad projection of their own weak character. Your ability to empathize will be heightened, and little that anyone says or does will hurt you.

Your power will carry you through whatever you undertake, just like Luke Skywalker's protective "Force." And while you may not always succeed, you will remain relatively unscathed in the process. Your projects may "fail" on a public level, not eliciting many sales or becoming critical hits, but for you they will always be sacred—that thing you did which you truly believed in and loved. And behind that failure will still be substantial joy and pride.

Best of all, you will know you are living as you were meant to live, at your maximum potential. The nagging thoughts of "I should" and "I really ought" will dry up and disappear as you move deeper and deeper into your correct place on earth. The work that lies ahead will no longer seem intimidating but something you look forward to ripping into with your chainsaw. And as you merrily smash conventions and see the ripple effect of your power at play, you will connect once again with that core happiness that has to do with your place on earth.

Whether you realize it or not, you were hard-wired for power long ago. And plugging into that power requires no more than simply letting go of the fear, deciding you're worth it, and doing that which comes naturally.

The small voice will tell you what to do—all you have to do is listen. Whether you know it or not, the Force is already with you.

try this...

Spend one week treating yourself as the truly powerful person you are. Get up an hour early each day and take the walk you've been meaning to take. While you are walking, connect with your spiritual guidance [see page 47], and choose an affirmation for yourself that confirms your sense of power. (One of my personal favorites is "It's safe to trust my power.")

At least three times during the appointed week, take yourself to a place that feeds your soul—a museum, a forest, a concert, any place that calls to you. Make a special point of taking care of yourself that week. Don't have the usual glass of wine every night, and see how much better you sleep. If you smoke or drink copious amounts of caffeine, make a decision to stop for the week. Nurture yourself with food that's actually decent for you. For one week, cut out junk food and venture into whole grains and fresh produce, and drink water for a change. Unplug the television and let your answering machine pick up the phone. Then, once your life is free of the usual distractions, make a point of doing the work you were meant to do for at least five of the seven days this week.

At the end of the week, take yourself out for a sumptuous meal and assess how your feelings of power have changed.

why you are here

IF THERE IS ONE FINAL THOUGHT I could leave you with, it would have to be this: Remember why you are here.

I would suggest that it is probably not so you can do the hang thing in front of old Seinfeld reruns, nor is it to compulsively keep house or to cruise catalogs. You and I both know there's something bigger on the Universal agenda for you, and you have already been called upon many times to fan those smoldering embers. Otherwise, you probably wouldn't be reading this book.

Well, I'm telling you once again: Make a fire, and this time, let it rage.

Your purpose in life is sacred territory; it is the beloved idea you wish you could get to if you just had the time, the project you started once but stopped when it scared you. Your purpose in life is not necessarily that useful, responsible, taxpaying thing you do every day from nine to five. It is bigger than that, for it is predicated on what pours from your soul when you bother to open it up. And it demands every ounce of courage, love, sweat, and perseverance you've got. Your purpose in life remains in the hands of God—until you decide to live dangerously and reach for it.

There are no guarantees what the results will be, for purposes aren't always necessarily about results. Your purpose in life may actually be to start restaurants that fail. But you must start them, and so go through all the marvelous crenelations of that process, in order to grow in the ways you were intended to grow.

This purpose business is, in fact, not about the fulfillment of anything more than your own private destination as a person in this lifetime.

Therefore, it's the quality of the ride that counts, not whether you "get there" or not. I even question whether there really is a "there," for the act of creating is, in and of itself, such a splendid, soul-enriching thing to begin with. So, in other words, create what you envision, and then toss it out into the world. If it catapults you to huge financial reward and screaming success, if Oprah, Phil, and the rest of the world clamor for interviews, then that's basically gravy, for your project will have already provided you with the fat steak of fulfilling your vision.

Dream your dream, and then dare to stake a claim in it. What you will receive in return will be all the riches of the world—yourself, as originally intended.

how to make time
for your soul

- **Unplug your television.** Even better, completely remove it.
- **Cancel your subscriptions.** Get rid of anything you don't read.
- **Make regular "soul" time every day.** If you're a morning person, get up one hour earlier and dig into your projects. If you're a night person, stay up one hour later.
- **Say no to your boss.** Leave at 5:00 or 5:30. Chances are, you'll find you're more valuable than you thought you were. Also, you'll probably find you work with increased efficiency. Offer to come in one hour earlier, if need be, to leave time for your evening classes, projects, or events.
- **Don't waste your lunch hour eating.** Bring a lunch to work, eat it briefly at your desk, and then get out there and do what really matters to you.
- **Stop agreeing to do things you don't truly want to do.** This includes volunteering, meeting friends and family, and serving on committees.
- **Redesign your work schedule.** Create one day or several afternoons a week to concentrate on the things you really want to do in life. Explore flex-time alternatives in your workplace. Consider telecommuting, working from a home office, or going free-lance with your company.
- **Put the kids to bed earlier.** Establish "grown-up" time, a time zone when all your children are in bed (even if they're only looking at books or listening to tapes, before going to sleep) and the adults get to have a little room to breathe.

- **Multi-task it.** Fold nurturing practices into your routine, such as meditating while you walk, or practicing an instrument while dinner cooks. Rather than stare at work on the train, take a book you've been wanting to read. Books on tape are especially good for this.
- **Rethink your routine.** Jot down your daily routine, then reevaluate it. Does reading the newspaper cover-to-cover do as much for you as working on the furniture you keep wishing you had time to refinish?
- **Cut corners cooking.** Take advantage of gourmet take-out and grocery-store fast foods, such as prewashed salad, precut vegetables, and pre-marinated chicken.
- **Let the answering machine pick up.** Better yet, get on-line and encourage friends to e-mail you instead of calling.
- **Create your own sanctuary.** Make a room of your own, preferably with a door. Hang a "Do Not Disturb" sign on it, and don't let others interrupt you. Family and friends will honor your request to have some time for yourself only if you do, too.
- **Quit volunteering so much.** Cut your list back to only those things that truly enrich you. Give other people a chance to do the rest.
- **Divide up the housework.** Hand over the laundry and vacuuming to your mate. Teach your children to do dishes, cook meals, and mop floors. And be willing to give up control of the end results. Read Patricia H. Sprinkle's book, *Children Who Do Too Little: Why Your Kids Need to Work Around the House (and How to Get Them to Do It)* for terrific pointers on how to make this happen.
- **If you can't relax your standards, delegate.** Hire local teenagers, professional housecleaners, or even a temp service to help you clear out your desk, answer correspondence, pay bills, organize closets, walk the dog—whatever you can give up that makes more time for you.

- **Do something you truly love.** Once you've created this time for yourself, use it wisely. Take on the challenges and dreams that really will improve your life. Chances are that once you start, it will be very hard to stop.

a list of inspiring books

This randomly chosen list of books contains all kinds of different takes on work, spirituality, and the pleasures of being your own person.

Mastery: Interviews with Thirty Remarkable People.
Joan Evelyn Ames. Portland, Ore.: Rudra Press, 1997.
In-depth interviews with highly successful people like Marilyn Horne, Henry Louis Gates Jr., financier J. Peter Steidlmayer, and juggler Michael Moschen about exactly how they have achieved mastery of their crafts.

Conversations with God: An Uncommon Dialogue. [Book One.]
Neale Donald Walsch. New York: Putnam, 1995.
Excellent spiritual insights into how to live the life you want to live.

The Artist's Way: A Spiritual Path to Higher Creativity.
Julia Cameron. New York: Tarcher/Putnam, 1992.
Ideas and exercises for discovering your artist self. This book is the established classic in this relatively new area of self-help. Also contain methods for starting your own Artist's Way groups and salons—an excellent support tactic.

If You Want to Write.
Brenda Ueland. St. Paul, Minn.: Graywolf Press, 1987.
My favorite book about writing—written years ago but still as fresh, true, and insightful as ever. Very good for getting over yourself.

The Nature of Personal Reality: Specific, Practical Techniques for Solving Everyday Problems and Enriching the Life You Know.
Seth (Spirit), [channeled by] Jane Roberts. San Rafael, Calif.: New World Library, 1974.
If you can get over the fact that this book was channeled (i.e., delivered through the slightly tipsy person of Jane Roberts after she went into a trance), there's much to be gotten from it. Contains no small wisdom about the nature and power of our thinking process.

The Spirited Walker: Fitness Walking for Clarity, Balance, and Spiritual Connection.
Carolyn Scott Kortge. San Francisco: HarperSanFrancisco, 1998.

Prayer-Walking: A Simple Path to Body-and-Soul Fitness.
Linus Mundy. St. Meinrad, Ind.: Abbey Press, 1994.

Two great books that teach you how to take walks and meditate at the same time. Both very motivating.

The Wealthy 100: From Benjamin Franklin to Bill Gates—
A Ranking of the Richest Americans, Past and Present.
Michael Klepper and Robert Gunther. Secaucus, N.J.: Carol, Citadel, 1996.

Fascinating tales of trials, tribulations, unbelievable luck, and fortitude behind the richest Americans in history. Not a few rags-to-riches immigrant stories that will stir the soul.

The Path: Creating Your Mission Statement for Work and for Life.
Laurie Beth Jones. New York: Hyperion, 1996.

Provides an effective way to access your own, all-important mission in life. Perfect for those who can't make up their mind.

In Honor of Women: A Revolutionary Approach to Preventing Breast Cancer and Other Diseases.
Stella Togo Crawley. New York: Ballantine Books, 1998.

An important book by a breast-cancer survivor on exactly how to give yourself the time and nurturing you need to really live full-out. Powerful stuff, whether or not you consider yourself a candidate for this disease (more than 75 percent of breast-cancer cases occur in women with no risk factor). Just a great book about womanhood.

acknowledgments

WHILE IT APPEARS THAT I WROTE THIS BOOK, in a curious way I didn't. I just sat down one day to noodle around with "something inspirational" and an entire book poured through me at lightning speed. The manuscript was completed in just under two weeks. That said, the obvious acknowledgment here should be to God, who was clearly the source of this material.

However, during the ensuing two years I spent finding the publisher for this book, I got great help and support from the following people who helped me refine and improve it. I wish to thank Margie Livingston, Michael Levine, Alex Forbes, Dr. Robert Akeret, Vicki Psihoyos, Tom Kulaga, Dolly Shivers, Henry Dunow, Marcia Menter, Laurie Dowdeswell, Kathryn Reinhardt, Dick Bond, Andrea Costa, and the participants in the "How Much Joy Can You Stand?" workshops.

I would also like to acknowledge Sari Botton, Amelia Sheldon, Cynthia Black, and the Beyond Words staff for helping me bring this book to fruition, and Lottchen Shivers and Fauzia Burke for their sage marketing advice.

Finally, I thank my husband, Larry Barns, and my children for their interest, support, and total faith in my work.

about the author

SUZANNE FALTER-BARNS is a novelist and writer of inspirational books. She is the author of a novel, *Doin' the Box Step*. Her articles and essays have appeared in *Self, Fitness, Adweek,* and *The New York Times* Op-Ed page. She also lectures and leads workshops on inspiration and creativity and has taught writing at The New York University School for Continuing Education. She has had careers as a cabaret singer/songwriter, copywriter, and psychic healer. She is a graduate of Wellesley College.

author's workshops
and web site

"HOW MUCH JOY CAN YOU STAND?" is a one-day workshop whose purpose is to reignite your creative spark—to fuel, feed, excite, and encourage the
small dreams we keep like secrets and never do anything about. The workshop uncovers and defuses the thousand good reasons why we never get
down to work and demystifies the creative process so you can tap into your
own spiritual resources.

Suzanne Falter-Barns is also available as a public speaker and consultant.
For more information and a schedule of workshops and appearances, please
visit the "How Much Joy Can You Stand?" Web site at *www.howmuchjoy.com.*

beyond words publishing, inc.

Our corporate mission:

Inspire to Integrity

Our declared values:

We give to all of life as life has given us.

We honor all relationships.

Trust and stewardship are integral to fulfilling dreams.

Collaboration is essential to create miracles.

Creativity and aesthetics nourish the soul.

Unlimited thinking is fundamental.

Living your passion is vital.

Joy and humor open our hearts to growth.

It is important to remind ourselves of love.

To order or to request a catalog, contact
Beyond Words Publishing, Inc.
20827 N.W. Cornell Road, Suite 500
Hillsboro, OR 97124-9808
503-531-8700 or 1-800-284-9673